SELF-REMEMBERING

SELF-REMEMBERING

ROBERT EARL BURTON

SAMUEL WEISER, INC.

York Beach, Maine

This edition first published in 1995 by
Samuel Weiser, Inc.
Box 612
York Beach, ME 03910-0612

03 02 01 00
10 9 8 7 6 5 4 3

Library of Congress Cataloging-in-Publication Data
Burton, Robert E.
     Self-remembering / Robert Earl Burton.
          p.   cm.
     Previously published: Yorktown, NY : Joel Friedlander, 1991.
          1. Uspenskiĭ, P. D. (Petr Dem 'ianovich), 1878-1947--Teach-
ings. 2. Fourth Way (Occultism). 3. Self-consciousness.
4. Awareness.
I. Title.
[BP605.G9B87   1995]
197--dc20   95-16125
                                                                  CIP

ISBN 0-87728-844-5
TS

Printed in the United States of America

The paper used in this publication meets the minimum requirements of the American National Standard for Permanence of Paper
for Printed Library Materials Z39.48-1984.

This book is dedicated to my beloved students,
both living and deceased, who are more than I could ask for;
I could not ask for so much.

Love, Robert

CONTENTS

INTRODUCTION

Twenty-five years ago, Robert Earl Burton founded the Fellowship of Friends, a school of spiritual development in the Fourth Way tradition, which has been transmitted in this century by G. I. Gurdjieff and P. D. Ouspensky.

A Greek-Armenian mystic and teacher of sacred dances, Gurdjieff rediscovered the Fourth Way tradition during long travels in the East, which provided the inspiration for his book, *Meetings with Remarkable Men.* He is perhaps best known for *Beelzebub's Tales to His Grandson.* Gurdjieff's principle disciple, Ouspensky, became a teacher in his own right, and recorded the Fourth Way ideas in a series of clearly written and elegantly reasoned works, among which are *The Fourth Way* and *In Search of the Miraculous,* both published after his death in 1947.

One characteristic of the teaching as expounded by Gurdjieff and Ouspensky is the use of a specialized language to ensure precision and understanding among its students. Some ordinary words have been given new meanings, and readers are urged to consult the glossary at the end of the book for any terms that are unfamiliar or confusing.

Because the Fourth Way is based on individual verification and understanding, as well as on personal transmission, each teacher reinterprets it anew. Robert Burton's teaching, while based on the knowledge transmitted by Gurdjieff and Ouspensky, has expanded to embrace the legacy of spiritually developed men and women of all ages and cultures, from Marcus Aurelius and St. Paul to Lao Tzu and Abraham Lincoln. Gurdjieff approached the Fourth Way through the rigorous physical training of his sacred dances, and Ouspensky emphasized an equally rigorous intellectual discipline. Robert Burton stresses the education and disciplining of the emotions. The unique

qualities that he offers to his students include a love of beauty
and an understanding of its capacity to create higher states of
awareness, a non-judgmental acceptance of people and events as
they are, and a profound humility and obedience in the face of
a higher intelligence. "If I had three wishes," he once said, "they
would be: Thy will be done, thy will be done, thy will be done."

Perhaps Robert Burton's greatest contribution to the Fourth
Way tradition is his unerring ability to grasp the core of the
teaching. Although the system offers an array of theories, he has
resisted all temptations to deviate from its highest application:
the creation of higher consciousness within its students. He has
never ceased to repeat that this work is simple, although it is
not easy. Out of the great storehouse of knowledge in the Fourth
Way, he has extracted and exalted two principles above all others: self-remembering and the transformation of suffering.

Self-remembering is the attempt within a specific moment
to be more conscious, more aware, more *present*. It is a form of
active meditation that may take place in any moment and in
any situation, in which the student works to be aware both of
himself and of his environment simultaneously, rather than
being immersed in his internal world, or lost in his reactions to
the many stimuli around him. Repeated efforts to self-remember lead to higher states of consciousness, and a quite new
understanding of humanity's place in the universe. This private, internal struggle to witness one's own life is the process
through which one creates one's soul.

Relentlessly, Robert Burton has placed self-remembering at
the heart of his school. Although he has urged his students to
experience the best that life can offer and to develop their own
talents and skills, he has never lost sight of the fact that even
great genius pales before simple consciousness; that, as he has
said so often, "there is no greater activity than presence in
silence."

The transformation of suffering entails learning to use each
negative or painful experience or emotion, whether large or
small, to create self-remembering. This process requires long
work on changing attitudes, so that the student understands

that the ultimate responsibility for any negative emotion—anger, irritation, fear, self-pity, and so on—rests with the individual rather than the events that befall him. "Everyone suffers, with or without a school," Robert Burton has said. "We are trying to use our suffering, rather than being used by it."

Year after year, Robert Burton's students have come to him with their questions, their problems, their protests. Year after year, with unfaltering patience, he has taught that the only true solutions to any perceived "problem" lie in our efforts to self-remember and to transform our suffering. However justified one's complaints, however unjust the events of one's life, one has no choice but to embrace them all. This wider acceptance is the key to the actual transformation of negative emotions into higher consciousness, which creates the capacity for selfless love and is the true meaning behind every spiritual teaching. What the individual gains through this process may then be radiated outward for the benefit of others. "There is a secret," Robert Burton said once, "that is almost too sacred to tell. The secret is: what one gains, all gain."

In the years since its founding, the Fellowship, which is based in northern California, has slowly and quietly grown to include approximately two thousand members in teaching centers around the world (for a partial list of such centers please turn to page 217 of the book). It is sincerely hoped that this book will not only serve as a record for Robert Burton's students, but will introduce others to their own spiritual possibilities.

This book is the result of efforts by many Fellowship members over many years. Not everyone can be thanked individually, but special mention must be made of the substantial contributions from Elizabeth Evans, Linda Kaplan, Catherine Searle, and Brunella Windsor. Also gratefully acknowledged are Girard Haven, who undertook the task of creating the glossary, and the translators who labored to produce faithful versions of this book in several languages.

—Jeanne Chapman
Apollo, California

Not one of you has noticed the most important thing that I have pointed out to you, that is to say, not one of you has noticed that you do not remember yourselves... Remember yourselves always and everywhere.

George Gurdjieff

Effort to remember yourself is the chief thing, because without it nothing else has any value; it must be the basis of everything.

Peter Ouspensky

When one begins to see that one can only begin to remember oneself for seconds at a time, it seems negligible, but what one must understand is that it is difficult exactly because it is the beginning of a *new state* for us, the key to a new world. If it were easy and if results came more quickly it could not have the importance which it has.

Rodney Collin

SELF-REMEMBERING

BEING PRESENT

There is no greater miracle than being present. Everything begins and never ends from this.

What does the term self-remembering mean? It means that your dormant self is remembering to be awake.

Endings are an illusion, because the present is eternal. To be present where one is is the simple story of one's life.

Each inconspicuous moment *is* our life; just sitting, trying to be present.

It's difficult to be present, yet throughout our life everything remains uncertain except the present. We look to the future, thinking there is more there than here. Man bypasses the present by pursuing the elusive future or dwelling on the past. What we should want is the present, but what the machine wants is anything but the present. We have to keep endlessly retrieving the present—we have dedicated our lives to that.

You can't be present at your destination if you're not present *en route.*

When I have 'I's that wish to be somewhere else, I have learned to immediately convert them into being present, because the machine is never satisfied with where it is. In a way, we're fortunate that the 'I's repeat themselves and are so clearly insubstantial. They make the substance of life obvious, because the most absurd things will try to take us away from the present. The more absurd they are the better, because then we know there's no point in pursuing them.

The machine cannot be present, so it searches for alternatives; that is its lot. Although the machine is usually displeased with the present, this day is as important as a day thirty years from now—at least today is certain.

An interesting 'I' came during the concert: "What do you want?" And the answer was, "Just to be present, that is all." Nothing compares with self-remembering and nothing truly exists without it. Sometimes, with self-remembering, everything one sees turns into poetry, echoing heaven: the flowers, the light falling on the grass. Just think how many subtle shades of green there are in nature.

Our dinners are like being on a ship at sea—there's nowhere to go, and we just settle down into the present. One of the most enjoyable aspects of dining together is being here and not having the machine discontented with the moment, not wanting to be anywhere else. The four lower centers are more agreeable now to the presence of something higher. Consciousness has degrees, and our consciousness is higher now than perhaps at any other time today. We are still trying to be present, and this moment will never present itself again.

We haven't mentioned self-remembering tonight, but it consistently looms behind our actions. When one is trying to be present it doesn't matter if one is speaking about Rilke's *Duino Elegies* or a student's wheelchair, as long as self-remembering permeates one's actions. This is why the Fourth Way primarily occurs in the midst of ordinary life.

We work hard each day to be present, and you should never make light of your efforts at the end of a day. We have each done all we can for our self, our school and Influence C. We can't change events, but we can change ourselves. Focus without words; don't identify with events—transform them and be present.

Everything is relative and subjective except one's self. When one is present, one is objective; that is, one has no other object but one's self.

It is important to work diligently on being present, but not to press too hard, because you can stand in your own way. Do everything you can to be present, but don't become too tense because that is another way to thwart self-remembering.

What was the most important thing you learned on your recent journey?
To be where I am—and to accept it. If I were not present when I travel, there would be no need to travel, because there is truly nowhere to go but the present. When one travels one objectively witnesses the subjectivity of man.

We receive our share of joy and happiness, but these are not the aim. We are here to be present, which should make us happy. Each moment offers the possibility of penetrating the present. You must use your time well, remembering that your time is counted.

How can one stop hurrying?
By realizing that the next moment is not greater than the present moment.

How can one keep from criticizing oneself about not being present?
Self-deprecation 'I's are not self-remembering. They are yet another waste of time and in reality reflect a lazy mind.

Emotional upheavals provide an opportunity to be present and make progress. While you are experiencing a strong negative emotion, remember that it will subside. We often wish we had remembered this during, rather than after, the storm. You do not exist when negative emotions engulf you. Also, remember that the noble king of hearts is designed to fail eventually so that your divine higher centers can emerge.

Some shocks are so incomprehensible that one is forced to turn to self-remembering. One's immediate impulse is to be present, and self-remembering becomes self-defense. Johann Goethe said, "He who seizes the moment is your man." *You* need to seize the moment—or something else will.

Try not to twist the present into something it is not; accept it on its own irrefutable terms.

Plutarch said, "The present offers itself to us only for the second and then eludes the senses." The present eludes the senses because consciousness is not functions. Our higher centers are not of the senses, but we try to use the senses to create higher centers. Just looking at an arrangement of flowers, remaining aware of your self, produces higher centers.

Home is where one is present. When I returned from my trip, self-remembering became very familiar, but I knew in the core of my being that the state, not the location, was to be treasured.

We do not think about the person we were before we met the school, because we aren't that person anymore. Indeed, there was no one present then.

Just trying to be where one is in this moment is self-remembering. Controlling one's mind, which is prone to wander, is an expression of remembering oneself.

One gains many treasures as one changes one's level of being, and the greatest treasure is the ability to penetrate the present more frequently and deeply. One can have everything if one is content with the present, nothing else is as exciting. There is a great victory to be attained, and we are winning.

The present is eternal.

One reason it is so difficult to remember ourselves is because the present is so near to us. We rarely look in front of ourselves for what we are seeking.

In certain respects I have a terrible memory—from trying to be present and not in the past or future. Many things are forgotten, but this is a small sacrifice compared to being present. We don't sacrifice anything of value when we try to awaken—death is the miserable lot of life, but all the moments in which we penetrated the present are indestructible. As for the rest, it is only wasted time. I try not to be enticed by reminiscence. When pleasant or un-pleasant memories try to occupy the living present, one can glance at them for a few seconds, or ignore them, and then return to the present.

Our lives are no more than each step we take and each moment that passes, but our machines persist in thinking that life should be other than the present. At times I pause, and wherever I find myself, in familiar situations or unusual ones, I think, "The events of this day constitute my life." Behind all questions looms the enigma of how to be present, and the greatest happiness for a rational man is the ability to be present to his own life.

This moment offers as many possibilities as any other time of the day, or any other time in your life. You must work well with whatever the present offers. Don't be deceived—the next moment is not of greater value than the present one. Indeed, you can't experience the future without penetrating the present, for the present *is* the future.

Each age offers the present, which is all it can ever offer. How sweet and clear the present is; how perfectly contented it is with itself.

Ironically, one can add to one's false personality if one acquires the *act* of self-remembering, rather than self-remembering itself.

As the years go by one lives more and more for each day, and self-remembering and friendship become the ultimate achievements. Horace said, "Happy the man and happy he alone who can call today his own."

One of the best ways to be present is to listen. As I was listening to the music and working with self-remembering, no useful thoughts came along until an 'I' said, "It is enough to be present."

William Shakespeare's statement, "To be or not to be," is composed of six words, five of which contain only two letters. This economy of language represents the idea that awakening is an essential process. The highest dimension of being occurs when one's self remembers *to be*.

Truly, we can go nowhere but the present; the moving center can take us to a place that is refreshing, but we can go nowhere but the present. Omar Khayyam wrote, "And lo, the phantom caravan has reached the Nothing it set out from—Oh, make haste!"

Tonight is not a bridge to anything, tonight is itself. The words we have spoken don't lead us anywhere but to the present.

Self-remembering means embracing the present, whatever it contains; that would mean tasting one's wine or looking at the beautiful arrangement of white tulips. Mr. Ouspensky said that "all the ideas of the system revolve around this one idea." Self-remembering is the hub of the wheel, all the other ideas are spokes.

Influence C has cast us together—let us try to enjoy ourselves. Anyone can be in imagination, anyone can be despondent, anyone can be negative. Try to avoid imagination, identification, negative emotions. We have the present.

Johann Goethe had a remarkable life, and is a conscious being. He completed his task on the first day of spring, symbolizing that he had found the eternal fountain of youth. During his last days, he seemed to an observer to be free of many illusions and to no longer live for the future or the past, but in the lucid present.

The purpose of meditation is to be present, and being present is not reserved for special occasions or special environments; it must occur wherever one is, regardless of one's circumstances.

One definition of success is being present as much as you can each day. You also must measure how much you were able to externally consider others. Take this idea simply, as all profound ideas are simple. If two people are passing through a door, and you choose to be the second to pass through it, you have been externally considerate. A day is a long unit of time, and there are many small opportunities like this to apply the different tools of the system. External consideration is one work tool; you can be using it, and a moment later be struggling with keeping accounts against the same person. Our lives are composed of moment-to-moment struggles to be present and we grow in proportion to our ability to give, which is why conscious beings are characterized by compassionate actions that elevate humanity.

There is no greater activity than presence in silence—it cannot be imitated.

Whole groups of 'I's on alluring subjects try to draw one away from the present.

Everything but the present is illusion.

Most men think they don't have time to be present; they imagine that it's designed for special circumstances. Try to be where you are and not allow the past to permeate the present. The past is but a word, while the present is a shifting reality. You can only leave the past through the present, and through the present you work for the future. Our work is always now. We have nowhere to go but the present, for all roads lead to the living moment.

Relentlessly focus on the present as best as you can. If it is a few seconds or a moment each day, be grateful. The present need not be more, nor other, than it is. As we grow older, we have to separate from our inability, at times, to be present. One of the best ways to be present is to separate from the disappointment that comes from realizing we have not been present. Our hearts are so resilient.

When I first started to be present, I couldn't speak and be present at the same time. It took a while to be able to do that. When self-remembering began appearing, I didn't concern myself with which state it was, I just let it be and experienced it. I did not want to be pulled away from it. I wish nothing more than to be present in this moment.

Keep returning to the present. The only realizable idea on the earth is being present, it's truly the only thing possible, and it is not mechanical.

As long as one can breathe it is time to remember oneself. One's self—this common word belies the incredible nature of the achievement.

Can you tell us what we need to do to be present?
You have to find the environment more interesting than imagination.

How can I work with identification that keeps me from being present?
One trades identification for one's identity. This lovely system works, but only if we use it. The system doesn't flatter us, but it enables us to escape.

It is important to fill centers, but not as important as being present.

Be grateful for the present.

Will—that is the best power, and the rest is just mechanics. Will is self-remembering, and being present is will power.

Is prayer useful?
Yes, if you ask for the right thing: help from Influence C to awaken, which almost certainly will mean transforming suffering.

We will be trying to be present until our last breath. With self-remembering, you don't have to wait to experience eternity, because eternity is here when you are present.

Bernard Berenson, traveling through southern Italy in his ninetieth year, spoke of the beautiful views he was beholding. "What views of Ischia, of Procida, of more distant cameo-like Capri! Die alte Weise, how it grips me still, but it is the grip now that counts and not the message. Indeed, there is no more message. It is IT. IT is its own and only purpose. IT is intransitive."

You must reach a point where you stop expecting to receive messages about being present. You must grip self-remembering and stop talking about it; you must be present!

SELF-REMEMBERING

It's not easy to discuss self-remembering because, in its highest form, it is a non-verbal process. Self-remembering is an idea that had never actually surfaced under its own name until the twentieth century.

We all remembered ourselves before we met the system, but we did not know what to call it and, more importantly, we did not value it. When one is remembering oneself, one is also creating one's self—creating an astral body. Our lives are composed of so many common moments, so many common miracles. A great part of self-remembering is recognizing the sublime within the common. We have to remember to appreciate the simple and unheralded nature of self-remembering. It is the opposite of life, which clamors for our *undivided* attention.

Mr. Ouspensky said that one cannot know one's position by oneself; one must be instructed. One must be led to understand that the hidden meaning of life on earth is to create a soul through the indefatigable process of self-remembering. He also said that we must realize we have discovered the weak point in the walls of mechanicality, the "Achilles' heel" of the machine. The primary idea this system offers is self-remembering, an idea completely overlooked by Western psychology. In all of Western culture, it is only in literature that we encounter the concept of penetrating the present.

One of the best ways to work on self-remembering is to remove what is not self-remembering. Paradoxically, one must be remembering oneself in order to do this. Also, do not seek a single definition of self-remembering, because it is many things. Self-remembering has passed under various beautiful names in different centuries. William Shakespeare said, "A rose by any other name would smell as sweet." History has produced many other men who are immortal, but who never heard the term "self-remembering."

We are involved in something both joyful and unpleasant. The separation from these two experiences, not the indulgence in them, gives one life. Self-remembering is the only activity on the earth that is not biological.

We cannot understand self-remembering in thirty minutes, and what it entails can't be described in one day. Self-remembering is the great mystery of organic life on earth, and one should not expect objective wisdom, which has been hidden for centuries, to be easily understood.

Self-remembering is an eighteen-hour-a-day endeavor. One must be working with some obstacle each hour of the day, and if it isn't non-existence or power, it will be imagination, inner considering or identification. There is no substitute for self-remembering, and that is difficult news as well as good news.

The intellectual center shares experiences by speaking about them, since language is its only medium of communication. And so we must use words to penetrate a divine, wordless state. Mr. Ouspensky reminds us that self-remembering is not mind activity, and that knowledge cannot be a substitute for self-remembering. The proper function of our intellectual center is to describe and classify phenomena, although the descriptions we give to objects are not the objects themselves. When this activity hinders self-remembering, it is wrong work.

Men number four must limit the time they think about ideas, because self-remembering readily disappears behind words. Harriet Beecher Stowe advised people to stop thinking, and be content to *be*, and indeed, taking in the impressions about one can be miraculous enough.

Formatory mind tries to reduce a subject to one all-embracing statement. It desires one definition of self-remembering, as though one's higher centers were a limited experience, but self-remembering has many facets. Taste the wine, look at the flowers, hear the music. It is strange that it is always quite close, although it assumes many forms. It is external consideration, non-identification, non-expression of negative emotions, voluntary suffering and, above all, the transformation of suffering. Each of these experiences is a hue of self-remembering. One's self may also be evoked during moments of danger, and amidst great beauty.

One way to find out what self-remembering is, is to find out what it isn't. Through a similar procedure you can verify your chief feature, body type and center of gravity. If you remove some of the variables, there are fewer left to examine.

Omar Khayyam said, "One thing is certain... and the rest is lies." Self-remembering is the eternal truth that masterfully confronts the eternal lie.

Mr. Ouspensky observed that we are accustomed to unreality. Mr. Gurdjieff entitled one of his last works *Life is real only then, when "I am."* For us and for him this means that life is real only when one is remembering oneself.

Self-remembering has no momentum; one must make effort, moment to moment. When the third state appears, experience it instead of simply talking about it—it is your self, your soul, Mendelssohn's "Song Without Words."

You cannot talk your way out, or eat your way out, or laugh your way out, or cry your way out; but you can remember your way out. Remember yourself a little at a time.

If you are remembering yourself and other people can't see it, then you're remembering yourself successfully. If false personality acts as if it is self-remembering, you are diminishing yourself.

Human nature generally does not see the obvious, which is why esoteric truths have frequently been presented in the form of fairy tales. Fairy tales often begin with the statement, "Once upon a time," indicating that the stories are unfolding in time, and end with a prince and a princess (World 6 and World 12) living "happily ever after," that is, in eternity—immortality.

The development of one's level of being is proportionate to the maturity of one's king of hearts. Self-remembering must originate in the king of hearts, because we can't rely on accidents to produce consciousness. We all need as much help as we can get, whether from our own efforts, the law of accident, or Influence C.

Dante Alighieri said that a tiny spark may burst into a mighty flame. The method to use is self-remembering. Yet there is nothing more elusive than self-remembering and we must, in our feeble way, return to it when we can. A neutral state is not a vegetative condition, but a state of non-attachment that repels imagination; it is a state of remembering oneself. The moments we vividly remember in our lives are the moments of self-remembering. Even so, self-remembering has degrees; if you are traveling in a foreign country, you may be present to hundreds of trees without remembering most of them. Where there is memory, where there is divided attention, there is your self.

Our moments of memory constitute our lives. If one reviews one's life, the moments one truly remembers reveal that one's higher

centers were present. Mr. Ouspensky said that of the other moments, we only know they occurred.

The Fourth Way provides a sound, basic structure for one's
evolution, and it can do no more, because self-remembering
cannot be imitated. Although most art one sees is imitative, there
is no imitating self-remembering. Nothing is full self-remembering but one's self, remembering.

There are certain memories in our childhood that time has not
eroded. Why is this? These moments are of the fourth dimension
and are not eradicated by the passage of time. Self-remembering
is the only phenomenon that masters both time and death.
Paradoxically, one of the best ways to prolong self-remembering
is by trying to not hold onto it. When unusual, productive states
emerge, try to elicit a work 'I' that says, "Let it be." You can
remember yourself more if you don't wish the moment to be other
than it is.

Self-remembering is its own reward. It is an unheralded, unsensa-
tional, immortal process. Each time you remember yourself, you
have produced a flash of eternity that will not perish, while
everything physical must eventually perish. We are foolish when
we value the tangible above the intangible. Self-remembering must
incessantly recommence throughout your life; it is always within
your grasp.

Although we do not meditate in our school, we do try to control
our minds, not under special circumstances, but under all circumstances and in each waking moment. Most people are content
with allurement, and one dimension of allurement is thinking that
controlling the mind is for special circumstances—one day a week,
or six hours a day. This is insufficient. When one meditates, one
tries to control one's mind. When should one *not* be trying to do
that?

Is it possible to evolve without self-remembering?
No—it is hard enough to evolve *with* it.

Moment to moment, one must separate from what is not self-remembering and, in this way, indirectly create one's self. Michelangelo said about sculpture that he removed what was unnecessary. It is the same with self-remembering. Our lives are like a sculpture from which we daily chip away the useless. We must be able to discriminate between sleep and awakening. The effort to awaken is expressed esoterically in "Snow White and the Seven Dwarfs." The dwarfs worked in labyrinthine mines and searched for gems, which are like moments of self-remembering because they gleam in the dark. It is useful to ask oneself, "Is this self-remembering?" If it isn't, discard it.

Mr. Ouspensky reminds us that self-remembering is always right action. The problem is to give this thought the correct scale. It is the greatest idea the system offers, and is independent of the form of either one's body or the school.

Almost all imagination is negative because it occupies the space of one's self. It's difficult to remember to *try* to remember oneself. Trying to remember oneself, however, is still not remembering oneself, although it is a more blessed place to be than sleep. Full self-remembering means that higher centers are functioning—the self remembers to be awake.

So many things are not self-remembering. The words, "Be present," are not the state, although that phrase is dear to us in our aim to awaken. If you are working on what is not your self, then you are working on your self. Try to remember that it can be done, and it has been done.

Self-remembering is not a sensation. William Blake said, "I look through my eyes, not with them."

Consciousness has degrees. When one is gripping the present, consciousness is divine. When one is negative and degrading oneself, consciousness is very low. Ridiculing oneself is not self-remembering, it's just a waste of time.

Feeling guilty about our good luck in having met the school—that, too, is not self-remembering. In right order, one is not affected by anything outside of oneself. It is curious that what we must call self-study is not actually the study of one's self, but the study of the machine's peculiarities. What one observes is not one's self, whether it is positive or negative. What observes is one's self.

Awakening is an emotional process and friction must be emotional. The suffering we experience must be real because the states we create are real. It isn't pleasant to verify this, and yet it is a blessing. Friction can seem like a curse until we begin to realize the great idea behind it. What is that great idea? Immortality. Can anything compare with that?

One needs to ask oneself, "Am I self-remembering?" If you are negative and you change the subject of your thought or conversation, you can observe that the machine will identify and become negative about the new subject with the same vehemence. So you have to control the source of negativity, and you learn to recognize the source by observing the subject. We understand self-remembering through trial and error.

Awakening is actually quite simple, although false personality wants to complicate it. Self-remembering is inconspicuous: one's higher centers are aware both of themselves and of the objects they view. Schools are for ordinary people with ordinary possibilities. And I was just thinking of this as we were dining—simple people, inconspicuously creating souls. The beauty of self-remembering is that it is independent of the subject and is always accessible to us.

Restoring the dead to life is the true meaning of self-remembering.

One can trust very little to memory. One of the reasons it is difficult to remember details is because we are trying to remember ourselves instead.

One needs external considering for a higher body to develop.

Our specialty is self-remembering. Because of this we are often average in other areas.

Never think any external action or achievement is more important than remembering yourself. Never consider the expression of negativity warranted. Try to bring self-remembering to small as well as large aims.

We have within us the beginning and the end of creation. Of the many observations one makes when one encounters the system, the strangest is that one must be taught to remember oneself.

What is the origin of tension in our machines, and how can it be used for self-remembering?
We live in a mechanical age that produces tension. There must be tension within one's machine to awaken. By promoting right work of centers, self-remembering diminishes tension. One can attempt to control the moving center by relaxing facial muscles, since a firmly closed mouth, which one rarely observes among infants, is an indication of tension.

Generally, self-remembering must originate in the intellectual part of the emotional center, because remembering oneself is an emotional experience. One can control the emotional center if one does not express negativity and, eventually, essence will displace negative emotions.

Try to avoid being asleep to daily miracles. Fortunately, one can produce being without knowledge. A certain number of years is required to understand the nature of self-remembering. One can only fully understand self-remembering when one's self remembers to be present. Our machines think that the experience of higher centers, and the transformation of suffering required to develop them, is reserved for someone else; it is, however, reserved for you.

The system has to be quite simple to reach us. The self is independent of the subject. Even work 'I's are not self-remembering. One of the beauties of self-remembering is that it can always appear regardless of the subject—it is a question of dividing attention.

Talking about self-remembering is not self-remembering. The system teaches us to transcend words.

One reason that eighty-five percent of our students work in life rather than at Apollo is that the more people around us are negative, the more opportunity we have to escape, because we are trying not to identify with the negativity. When one is really working, negative situations are a life-line.

I have been in the school a short time, and I cannot remember myself much.
As time passes you will be able to minimize what distracts you from being present, and your soul will gain strength. The more you remember yourself, the more you are able to remember yourself. After the first year in the teaching one makes better use of the second year; after the second, better use of the third.

Time appears to stand still when one is remembering oneself; in reality, one is moving at the fastest speed of all by simply being where one is.

What do I need to do?
When you eat, taste your food. When you listen, make your ears work and don't just let them hang around. Look with active, not passive vision. Your heart will lead you, and it knows what is right.

Affirmation of your aim to self-remember is the first force; the inertia of the machine is the second, or denying force; and the transformation of suffering is the third force.

The intellectual part of the intellectual center, the king of diamonds, is a timid instrument that we seldom use. Self-remembering, a creative process, demands its appearance. One's steward, in the intellectual part of the emotional center, draws upon the king of diamonds to awaken one's soul.

In the end, nothing stands between you and self-remembering but yourself.

My job is to get you to understand what I understand, what I have received from higher school. I have to transmit it repeatedly in order to eventually surpass words, because we seek a state, not words. The more one changes one's being, the more one concentrates on retrieving self-remembering and controlling centers. Speaking about self-remembering isn't enough, although even that is rare. One has to learn to value it above everything else and try to be the words. Speech is sometimes futile because consciousness is not functions. One needs to use words, but not too many. It is a delicate balance.

One can kill self-remembering in big or little ways; unnecessary talk kills it in little ways. Silence is our business, and it is where the real work must occur. One way to remember oneself is to listen to other people when they speak. Such a simple thought—but if it becomes a habit, it will change one's level of being. Let's hope they have something to say and don't make a short story long.

One of my favorite comments about self-remembering comes from Walt Whitman, although he didn't call it self-remembering. "And now the profound lesson of reception: neither preference nor denial." That is, just accept what each moment offers.

Self-remembering produces a unity of the intellectual parts of centers. The self is re-membered, regathered, and we are in a state of unity. Self-remembering must work with each simple moment because these are primarily what make up one's life. False personality may wait for large events and thoroughly fail.

Self-remembering is a very lean experience. When ideas become too complicated, false personality has entered one's work. Self-remembering is also a private experience, and although objective knowledge is not personal, the verification of it is quite personal. Self-remembering is not sensational; transforming negative emotions is not sensational; but through these efforts the "pearl of great price" is produced.

We are what observes and not what we observe—a happy thought. What observes one's machine is one's self, and what transforms suffering is one's self. Something without words quietly looks from one.

That which one truly possesses is without words, and peers from one's forehead. It is one's infant self, located between the holy temples in the pineal gland. No experience can compare to one's own awakening. The great truth amidst the great lie.

We have the keys to eternal life. I wish I could convey what a joke almost everything else is compared to self-remembering.

It amazes me that the ideas of the system remain so fresh.
Self-remembering is always fresh. For years I have been grateful to speak about one word—self-remembering—which means life or death for us. Self-remembering must be pursued inexhaustibly

throughout one's life. As we move toward death, we realize that all we can take with us is our selves.

Is giving thanks a form of self-remembering?
One cannot be thankless and remember oneself. In time, gratitude accompanies self-remembering. Near the end of his life Walt Whitman wrote: "For that O God, be it my latest word, here on my knees, old, poor, and paralyzed, I thank Thee."

No school in history has stressed self-remembering to the extent that our school has. We have made sure that the magnitude of the idea is not reduced by the abundance of other ideas, and we have set it higher than any other concept. There are five billion people on the earth, and it doesn't even occur to them to remember themselves, or their souls. One can see how benighted the minds of men are.

The pace for us quickens. The more one remembers oneself, the more one is able to remember oneself, because self-remembering is a cumulative process. We can introduce it at any time, and it cuts through everything to the very meaning of existence.

A beautiful way to think about self-remembering is, "Love that to which thou returnest"—the thread we return to throughout our lives. All things pass except one's self. Nothing is self-remembering but self-remembering.

George Kates, author of *The Years That Were Fat* and *Chinese Household Furniture*, was asked late in his life, at age ninety-four, if he missed China. He replied: "Don't think of me as being desirous of going back to China. The China I knew is no longer there. But the West I knew is no longer there either... I have no longing or homesickness for a world that's gone. It's gone for everybody. I could make a life of nostalgia for myself, but I regard that with distrust. We have a duty to live in the present, and I want to live on pleasant terms with it."

Finally, we are without words, and *we are*. Love is a powerful phenomenon, and the absence of self-remembering reveals an inability to love. The principal way one can assist others is by remembering oneself.

DIVIDED ATTENTION

Divided attention *is* self-remembering. You are what observes, not what you observe. What we look at is never real, but what looks through us, with divided attention, is real. When we divide our attention, we are a different order of creation, and higher worlds—World 6 or World 12—are working within us. We spend our life hauling a carcass around, trying to coerce divided attention out of it.

Anyone not in the business of building his soul is in the wrong business, because the only way to be truly employed is to be present. Divided attention is still the answer any day, in any century, and in any country. Tomorrow will be what today is; things never get better than the present.

The life of a student who has entered the way revolves around the effort to divide his attention.

To sustain self-remembering, one works on it every day of one's life. Never sacrifice divided attention for anything, because everything is secondary to dividing attention and creating a soul. Divided attention must accompany one throughout the day, regardless of the subject at hand. A student commented today on how much trouble he had been having dividing his attention the last three weeks. I told him that he probably hadn't been dividing his attention before, and was only now beginning to realize its difficulty.

Unfortunately, we are apt to be in imagination even while we are reading about, or listening to, work ideas. Our minds drift when we are not dividing our attention. We may be in imagination about something that occurred earlier today, or about a problem that may present itself tomorrow. One needs to employ the tool of inconspicuous voluntary suffering in order to avoid entering imagination. You can be discreet: take a slightly uncomfortable posture, sitting a little to the left on your chair, or a little to the right, or a little forward. Cross your legs if you normally do not. One must create many small shocks because there are so many small moments in one's life.

Trying to divide attention catapults one beyond the level of life. We are people who focus on divided attention as its own reward— it is our real specialty, but it will never be apparent to the mass of humanity. It is in the nature of self-remembering to be inconspicuous, but the results that it produces are profound.

Divided attention is our all and everything, the hidden meaning of life on earth. We are so wrapped up in our small worlds that we cannot sense the greater worlds.

At a certain point in one's evolution everything is nonsense compared to divided attention. It is a joke to be distracted by anything, but the joke is on us. If distractions get too serious, they are a bad joke.

Never sacrifice divided attention to anything, because everything is a lie except divided attention. The five billion people on the earth are not trying to divide attention. When I watch sporting events where 100,000 people happily lose themselves, I sometimes think, "Just try to interest these people in divided attention." However, I have learned that people get what they want, and that those who want a school get a school.

I was speaking to a student today who was telling me he had a problem. I told him the only problem he had was dividing attention. I was talking with someone else who was having a difficult time with something small, but his real difficulty is dividing attention. Everything else is absurd because it disintegrates in time. The great secret is that self-remembering must occur wherever one is.

I don't necessarily think in terms of teaching, but in terms of retracing my steps, because they are lovely steps that lead to the stars.

We have everything we need—self-remembering and divided attention. How great they are, and how humble. If we don't become more simple and less pretentious, there is no reason to ascend.

Every moment is as valuable as our last day. Perhaps today we can nurse more divided attention out of our machines than when we are seventy.

Death sweeps everything away. That is why our moments of divided attention are so precious—death cannot touch them. When we get older, cells in our body decline that were once vibrant and healthy. We are fortunate to discover divided attention, and to value it above everything else.

Questions won't necessarily help you divide attention. Once a student asked me too many questions, and I replied: "Remember that the answer is a state, not a question."

We are a microcosmos—man—and are the only beings on earth that can become twice born. As the caterpillar is mechanically reborn as a butterfly, so through divided attention we can be reborn consciously.

Divided attention does not yield immediate results, and higher centers cannot arrive without a persistent effort over many years. It is difficult to awaken, yet it can be done. One cannot awaken unless one makes a total commitment to one's evolution. If one thinks partial measures are sufficient, one is deceiving oneself.

Everything is a lie without divided attention.

Think of all the stops, halts, and pauses in your life, all the wasted time. A student traveling to other teaching centers asked if I had a message to send. I said, "No, there are no new messages, just divide attention."

One can verify that repeated attempts to divide one's attention bring fresh energy by observing an exhilaration when negative emotions subside.

Epictetus boldly said: "Show me the charm that can defeat death!" That charm is divided attention.

Children are in essence, but their essence is in a state of fascination. When *you* are in essence you try to divide attention. Try to look at these flowers and, at the same time, be aware that you are looking at them. Dividing attention puts one in essence. Christ said, "Except ye become as little children ye shall not enter into the kingdom of heaven."

Man cannot do. Humanity makes a gallant effort to do but everything it does is mechanical. How could humanity *do* without divided attention? Since people don't have divided attention, they are left floundering, and the more humanity thinks it can do, the farther it is from the truth.

When we see people perform well in life, their attention is concentrated, but not divided. What we seek desperately is divided attention, because if one is dividing attention, one's soul is present.

And under real stress, all philosophical wisdom gives way to the silent bearing of the ruling faculty—the soul, or higher centers. People pursue things outside of themselves rather than inside of themselves, which accounts for the many tragedies that we witness. It's astounding to see what captures our attention, yet everything must be secondary to dividing attention and creating a soul. What Influence C expects from us is divided attention, and that is what we will excel in—nothing else approaches it. We have to get beyond the subject matter to another message behind it. We are in a prison to the extent that we don't know it is a prison, and only divided attention can break through the walls.

Paul introduced divided attention to his followers when he said, "Behold, I show you a miracle, we shall not all sleep."

Humanity remains basically at the same level throughout the centuries and is busy going everywhere but the present. Humanity must remain under the law of accident because it does not know about self-remembering and dividing attention, and gives its energy away, chiefly by expressing negative emotions.

We are such privileged people. When one travels one cannot believe all the people one sees walking around without divided attention. But that's the way it is. And isn't it wonderful that we can divide attention? We have to strive for eternal life or fall into eternal darkness.

Humanity can't conceive that it serves as food for the Ray of Creation. The more men that exist on the earth, the worse it becomes, because as quantity increases, quality decreases. Humanity is the humus from which schools and conscious beings grow. It's strange to think that most people on earth have never encountered the phrase "divided attention."

How does self-remembering differ from divided attention?
Divided attention *is* self-remembering; they are synonymous. The state of divided attention encompasses a wide spectrum of emotions. Johann Sebastian Bach created some works that are characterized by profound emotions, whereas others are pastoral. In the same way, the soul has many hues.

Self-remembering means that one is aware both of oneself and of what one is viewing. If one views an object without being aware of oneself, one is in a state of fascination, which is one of the final barriers between sleep and higher centers.

One can be asleep while speaking about the system. It's an odd way to sleep, because it is close to the divine. Nevertheless, if one is not attempting to divide one's attention, regardless of the activity, one is asleep. Trying to control one's wandering mind while another is speaking can be a focal point for dividing attention, as the machine has a strong inclination to enter imagination at such times; that is its misguided way of being an active force. Epictetus said that man was given two ears and one tongue so that he might hear twice as much as he speaks. Also, when one cannot understand an idea after five or ten minutes, it can be profitably abandoned because it is occupying the space of divided attention. Matters will become less difficult if one can divide one's attention and observe impartially.

William Blake said: "The whole creation groans to be delivered." Everything in nature is driven to exist, but doesn't know where to go. We have unraveled the Gordian knot by discovering the secret of divided attention, and are using our energy to create an astral body.

When you have found the charm of mastering time—divided attention—you stop marking time and begin to defeat it. Time cannot erase your moments of presence. Because you are the microcosmos man, you must come to the point of death alone.

You are not the role you are playing, and each soul in the school is individual. Your soul will outlive the school because, through dividing attention, you can escape death.

Two things become apparent as one awakens. One, that there is truly no hope without divided attention, and two, how great is Influence C.

What time is not a good time to divide attention?

Results of
Self-Remembering

When intellectual types meet the system they often speak too much, just as emotionally-centered people can be too emotional. Although one must be emotional to awaken, self-remembering does not require an emotional center of gravity. When one enters the way, one penetrates essence and becomes truly emotional. Emotions that are not connected with self-remembering are not real.

If you would rule all, rule yourself.

Avoiding sentimentality doesn't make one insensitive; on the contrary, it makes one sensitive to finer states and more noble values.

Mr. Gurdjieff advised us that we need to create our own shocks. A little shock I have used for several years is to close doors by their handles, because mechanical parts of centers will use any part of the door. We can bring self-remembering to virtually anything if we wish to.

We need to remember that this system does not belong to us, as it is *objective* knowledge. Moments in which one's self remembers, which are the fruition of this work, are one's own. One makes the work one's own through efforts to remember oneself.

If one cannot evolve now when Influence C is so available, how can one evolve later under less favorable circumstances?

One of Mr. Ouspensky's most remarkable observations concerned his efforts to remember himself. He said, "The first attempts showed me how difficult it was. Attempts at self-remembering failed to give any results except to show me that in actual fact we never remember ourselves." Mr. Ouspensky was an exceptional man, and had a higher imagination of himself to relinquish than many people who meet the system. He had more than most people, yet he understood that without his self he possessed nothing. Although his first efforts were discouraging, he persevered and eventually fused his higher centers. He completed his role by becoming a full man number seven, leaving his physical body when it died and communicating with students who survived him.

To fill one's centers properly, one must make efforts to remember oneself. Fortunately, self-remembering begets self-remembering, just as culture begets culture. After one has been taught to self-remember, one proceeds to create one's self by self-remembering. Imagine the poverty of pursuing anything else; most people pursue Influence A rather than Influence C.

People without substance require novelty. Novelty sometimes evokes higher centers, but a man number four cannot rely upon it to create permanent consciousness. One needs to balance esoteric knowledge with general knowledge, yet avoid being carried away by intriguing thoughts. We do not deal with tantalizing philosophical or theoretical questions. One needs to intuitively subordinate these questions to the daily battle to be present.

Consciousness has degrees. One can verify that the machine is not real, and five minutes later another pseudo state can circulate within the machine that thinks *it* is real. As the weeks and months pass, one adds mass to one's being, and understands more deeply that the machine is truly insubstantial. One gains enough courage from such observations to be able to control one's machine, because one is confronting an illusion.

One's self, remembered, frees one from the law of accident. The law of accident can give one the opportunity to be creative if one is aware that it is occurring, because then one can decide whether to encourage or to resist it. One can only direct the law of accident, however, if one is remembering oneself.

Although we all study the same system, our efforts are quite personal. One reason to practice the looking and listening exercises is because they interrupt the over self-indulgence that arises from the machine's preoccupation with itself. Instead, one can be appreciating beautiful nature. Substantial being can be garnered, for example, by enjoying trees, as there are so many beautiful trees in this world. Appreciating nature and indeed, the entire Ray of Creation—galaxies, stars and planets—is a vital aspect of one's impressions octave. Walt Whitman wrote: "I was thinking this world enough until the stars appeared."

We frequently have to be reminded that the machine is a machine. Also, as we study this system, we can change our level of being and, with each change of being, we gain something permanent.

As we speak we are simultaneously trying to remember ourselves. There is a point in one's development where talking about self-remembering can become a barrier, but this doesn't mean one abandons the second and third lines of work.

If one self-remembers, one can observe errors in others and avoid making them oneself, just as one can know about a cold without having one. Galileo said his best teacher was watching the mistakes of others. What a breakthrough it is when our ears begin to hear and our eyes begin to see.

Our Renaissance soil is difficult to manage and, in a way, that is fortunate. Because results do not come easily, it builds character in the men and women that work it. Rodney Collin said that self-remembering is difficult precisely because it is the key to a new world. If results did come easily they would not be valuable.

If one has the aim to remember oneself, that is the first force; imagination poses a denying, or second force; friction brought by higher forces is a third force aiding the first force. When two forces oppose one's mechanicality, one's aim can be met; if one understands this, one understands the urgency of receiving outside help to awaken. Understanding this, one understands what to pray for. Omar Khayyam said: "And when the Angel with his darker Draught draws up to thee—take that, and do not shrink."

It is interesting how we develop the habit of saturating ourselves with culture: the concert, this room, the music, the impressions, all these hydrogens are higher hydrogens. From this we try to create self-remembering. Listening to music is generally a much more beautiful experience than listening to one's mind activity: the many 'I's.

It must be wonderful for you when you break through to self-remembering, even for just a few seconds. It shows everything else to be false, even though everything else, in the absence of self-remembering, seems true. Incredible, isn't? It is like Alice in Wonderland, traveling "through the looking glass."

I was thinking of the Pyramids. Even they are descending—pollution is slowly destroying them. But self-remembering is permanent, indestructible.

Remember, self-remembering is always right action, and one must cherish this thought. The system presents many ideas that seem to be opposed to one another and, without divided attention, knowledge can readily fall upon dualistic ears.

It is a blessing and a shock to grow old, and young, together. Self-remembering is the eternal fountain of youth that Ponce de Leon sought outside himself. We seek and find it inside ourselves. One meets a school and one's body becomes older, but essence starts to emerge and grow, and one is younger. The older students, older in age, look young because they have touched their own eternal fountain of youth—self-remembering.

Mr. Ouspensky said several things quite well that are exclusively for school ears. He said, "Remember yourself always and everywhere." That is, in the most ordinary circumstances, remember yourself. He also said that self-remembering produces definite chemical changes that herald the emergence of essence and, beyond that, of Worlds 6 and 12, Hansel and Gretel.

One observes that one cannot resist wrong work of centers all of the time unless one is awake all of the time. There are certain manifestations that cannot presently be controlled, because one must have some strength with which to control them. If one is not remembering oneself, how can one control centers?

I was shocked to realize that I didn't have even one 'I' to remember myself during the day.
You will reverse that someday and remember more often than you forget. It may take a series of lives, but you will prevail. Influence C is helping us and their aim is to make you immortal; they are not subject to the law of accident. When one understands this, one understands one cannot afford to compromise one's aim to awaken.

THE MACHINE

Self-remembering is a nuisance to the machine, which wants to be mechanical and waste time. The machine would rather have its wishes actualized than have them interrupted by self-remembering. Mr. Ouspensky advised us that false personality is opposed to self-remembering. Often, before people enter the way, false personality makes its last great assault, and one will be disoriented and beleaguered. In right order, false personality will shatter, and essence will emerge. It is a painful process, but it is the method by which many people enter the way.

The machine cannot remember itself because self-remembering is not mechanical. The whole Ray of Creation, organic life on earth, our bodies themselves, are all opposed to self-remembering. One's machine will cunningly convince one that self-remembering is occurring while the lower centers continue to pursue inferior aims. This deception must be taken into account, because awakening is mathematical. There is no way to escape death other than self-remembering.

Contradictions exist within our machines because we are not *one*. We have four brains: an intellectual brain, an emotional brain, a moving brain, and an instinctive brain. Our problem is further complicated because each of these brains has four subdivisions: an intellectual part, an emotional part, a moving part, and an instinctive part. Higher centers are unified, that is, they are the *state of unity*. If one verifies that one has four brains, one can understand that there must be contradictions that can be resolved by remembering oneself.

We learn to utilize negative 'I's by transforming them. Mr. Gurdjieff said we always make a profit. Work 'I's are excellent: "Divide your attention," "Be present." 'I's that are negative are useful if we don't identify with them and use them to be present.

Each of our four lower centers competes for space. It is as though we have one yard of soil in which to plant a redwood, a cedar, a cypress and a pine tree. Each tree is competing to win that yard of soil. And so it is with our four lower centers. Each moment their illusory lives are at stake.

The intellectual center is the weakest mind of the machine, and it is difficult to generate the desire to educate oneself. Some people lose self-remembering through resentment at having to fill their centers and educate their essences. Elizabeth I stated, "What you desire is of too great importance to be declared to a collection of brains so light."

To balance one's machine, one must be able to control centers which, in turn, requires remembering oneself. Balancing one's centers is common sense, which means a sense common to all four centers. The highest common sense is the sense of kings (intellectual parts of centers) acting in unison.

So much of our day is composed of our machines' wanton consumption of energy. Instead of employing one's mind for self-remembering, one's dull machine occupies space with a variety of subjects, depending upon which center has ascended.

It would be naïve to think that the self is easily attainable. Thus, one must personally understand how difficult it is to function from intellectual parts of centers. Controlling the queen of hearts, a somewhat insubstantial part of our being, is a useful task to establish for oneself. The emotional and mechanical divisions of centers are opposed to self-remembering, as they must be minimized for higher centers to ascend. Our enemies within are numerous and our possibilities of escape are limited without the outside assistance inherent in a conscious school. Christ said, "A man's foes shall be they of his own household."

How can one differentiate emotions of the queen of hearts from those of the king?
The subject of one's emotion indicates which part of the emotional center has ascended. Different subjects interest different parts of one's machine. If one is unhappy because of one's inability to remember oneself, then one can ascribe that pain to the king of hearts. If one is unhappy because of a relationship, identification has entered the queen of hearts.

Will the machine ever give up the idea that it is missing something?
We must remember that all 'I's are a substitute for self-remembering. The machine is always poised to undermine self-remembering, because a machine cannot remember itself. It cannot be present and so *it* often feels something is missing when *you* are present.

How can one work with the state of horror that is evoked by seeing one's condition more clearly?
Fortunately, these states do pass, usually after a few minutes. When one is frightened by observations of one's mechanicality, one's queen of hearts has ascended. The machine will attempt to use excessive fear to undermine one's work, and this, too, is not self-remembering. You can immediately correct the problem by remembering yourself.

Greed is insatiable, and is an unpleasant dimension of the emotional part of the emotional center. The queen of hearts wants merely to be wanting; that is one way she occupies space. If one satisfies her, she will wish something else within moments. The queen of hearts is characterized by a lack of relativity, and seeks instant gratification.

The queen of hearts is not useless; it is just not one's self. If divided attention accompanies it in a state of essence, it is adorable.

How can we accurately photograph sex energy?
The sex center is the depository for energy in the machine. It is a different order of creation than the other lower four centers. The sex center is a mechanism designed to refine materials, including the food one consumes, the air one breathes and the impressions one receives. It mechanically attends upon the four lower centers, yet its higher invisible purpose is to be utilized in remembering oneself. The sex center transforms hydrogens into finer energy, and through self-remembering the products of transformation enter the pineal gland, which Descartes called "the Throne of the Soul." Wrong work of centers misuses sex energy. It is difficult to photograph the sex center because it operates at such a high speed, but one way to detect it is by an increasing fervor in one's activities. For instance, if one is moving too quickly and feeling electric, sex energy has entered one or more centers. Generally this occurs because one has rested too much and has not made enough effort during the day. One can rid oneself of excessive sex energy by remaining awake longer. If one plans to retire at midnight, one can try to wait until 1:00 A.M. One can use sex energy for the four lower centers, or for higher centers, or both. We try to use it primarily for higher centers, and we make the highest use of sex energy when we transform negative emotions into an astral body. Most people use sex energy for procreation, which is an incredible expression of the sex center, and of the other centers as well. Procreation is, in a sense, sublime; sublime to the point that the vast majority of mankind has little or no inclination to go beyond it to the divine. Sex, like religion, keeps man asleep. Sex has its place; an ascending soul may do well with or without it. The wise man uses it primarily to create his astral body.

If one is controlling imagination and the expression of negative emotion, one is transmuting sex energy, for one cannot resist these obstinate forms of mechanicality without self-remembering.

On one level the sex center is designed to perpetuate the species; on a higher level it is intended to ignite the pineal gland, the seat of the soul, by transmuting sex energy. Nature has endowed man with an enormous amount of sex energy, and we witness a similar design in nature when a huge number of seeds is cast from a single tree; each of those seeds could become a tree, yet few do. Generally, the sex center can only be photographed from higher centers, and even then it is a difficult process because of the elusive nature of that brain.

All of our manifestations are dependent upon the energy of the sex center. Higher centers, essence and personality require the energy of the sex center, as do negative emotions, imagination and identification. Thus our lives consist of a struggle to direct the energies of our sex center toward our higher centers. Sex energy can be used for physical union, transmutation, or both.

The more one speaks, the less possibility one has of actualizing what one is speaking of, because speech has a tendency to displace reality. We can teach by actions as well as by words. Be grateful that the words we share turn into being.

Do you think there is some intelligence behind the machine?
We do have an incredibly intelligent machine to work with that is rarely seen for what it is: a machine. Each center has its own intelligence. Man is often a good creation but does have his dark side, especially in the intellectual part of the instinctive center, the king of clubs. It will make itself look dull to fool us into thinking that it is not cunning. We must not underestimate it—the lower tries to consume the higher. No matter how hard the machine tries, it can't remember itself, and it will always try to stop us from being present even though it has nothing to gain from it. The

machine repeats itself to lull us to sleep, and we must never think that it has shown us all its deceptions. When someone is speaking it will take space by producing itches, or by formulating 'I's about what it wants to express, or by completing sentences for other people.

We can, to a certain extent, calm the beast in us by giving it food. We must also control the instinctive center by restricting it. No part of the instinctive center is interested in awakening. The king of hearts is the instrument designed to produce higher centers; the instinctive center is intended to protect the organism during its life on earth.

One's instinctive center will try to control the environment through unnecessary talk, as this manifestation occupies space.

Never underestimate the instinctive center—it is always poised to undermine self-remembering. The instinctive center attempts to destroy hope. One must know it before one can control it, which is a long study. There are few people who can begin to control the instinctive center, because it is evasive and difficult to photograph. Mr. Ouspensky stated that it can only be photographed when one is conscious or approaching consciousness. Controlling its manifestations requires the ability to *do* by controlling the law of accident.

Because one dines approximately 86,000 times in one's life—not including snacks—it is necessary to find ways to remember oneself while eating. Before one begins to eat is yet another time to self-remember, as one may lose oneself to the instinctive center. Eating often brings a positive energy to the machine, but eating in excess prepares the groundwork for inner considering to displace self-remembering. In the school we use dining to awaken. Being present to food is one of the few instances when the instinctive center is in favor of self-remembering.

The instinctive center feigns consciousness and thinks it can be the third state. Expecting the instinctive center to be able to experience the third state is like asking a cow to fly. Third state experiences belong to the astral body, or soul. But when one brings attention to food, one uses the instinctive center as a medium to produce self-remembering.

The instinctive center likes to put statues on graves, which gives the illusion of permanence. But even stone gives way to time. Self-remembering does not—it's the only thing that can foil death. Subjective methods of awakening are rooted within the instinctive center and are, in reality, that center's way of expressing itself.

The intellectual part of the emotional center contains a mechanism that can learn to appreciate beauty without identifying with it. It is fortunate that beauty touches us, but not at the expense of controlling our emotions.

The Bible says, "For now we see through a glass, darkly," which esoterically means we perceive the world through our body types, centers of gravity, alchemies and chief features; and yet perhaps the predominant influence that colors our vision is the culture in which we were raised. To see objectively is difficult, and yet possible. Clearly, objective knowledge is necessary in order to make objective observations, and such rare knowledge is the property of consciousness. Attaining the ability to view man's condition objectively is a long process, which is why schools are for good householders and not for insubstantial people.

One's chief feature is strengthened because one is afraid of other people, and so one acts powerful, vain or greedy as a buffer. Vanity is a strong feature in each person. One's machine will vainly occupy space because it wishes to be the mechanical active force in a situation. The more conscious one becomes, the less one will occupy space.

Chief feature is most anxious to classify its manifestations as favorable because its illusory existence may be jeopardized.

How can we observe chief feature?
You can only observe if you are remembering yourself. Chief feature will try to reduce others, especially if they are working on themselves. If we are not self-remembering, it does not wish those around us to remember themselves either. For instance, a person with a vanity feature will talk excessively to focus attention upon himself. There is no advantage or disadvantage to possessing this chief feature, or any other chief feature. A chief feature is designed to be transformed, through self-remembering, into something divine: your self. Thinking that you have the worst chief feature is a dimension of vanity. In addition, if you think you don't have a chief feature or can't find it, it is probably vanity.

We don't make direct progress against chief feature. There are pauses and regressions amidst forward movements, and chief feature takes its toll on our being for many years. Time is a necessary element to consider when we attempt to resist any area of mechanicality.

Chief feature occupies the space that rightly belongs to self-remembering. When one diminishes chief feature, regardless of which feature it is, essence ascends.

Isn't it wonderful not to have an impulse that wishes to be somewhere else? The machine can't be present, but here we are settled down into the present. We can speak about anything if we're present, because we try to have self-remembering moving behind speech. We don't use the word 'I' because the machine's favorite subject is itself.

Imitation is very strong in us. It's hard not to imitate the billions of people in the world, to go against imitation to awaken. Imitation is often harmless, but when we are asleep and don't realize it is happening, it is harmful. We have to find a way to say "no" to imitation.

One has to keep forcing oneself on the present because the machine just wants to sleep. One has to go through type, center of gravity, features and alchemy, and work on what comes. Self-remembering is separate from these aspects of our mechanicality.

The knowledge we share is volatile, and one's machine will react to it by trying to secure its illusions more desperately.

The machine speaks and moves, but without self-remembering, it is only a moving illusion.

These machines are inventions of higher forces designed to remember themselves and to create souls. This vessel we have is truly a machine, and it does have a soul or ruling faculty.

If one cannot control one's machine, one *is* the machine.

FALSE PERSONALITY
AND ESSENCE

Problems and needs are the same for each person. Our problem is that we are in a machine; our need is to remember ourselves.

False personality is opposed to controls and restraints. To awaken you must wade through much imaginary denying force in your life, struggling with the weaknesses each moment presents. You can only be as effective as the effort you make.

False personality does not think simple situations are important enough for self-remembering. One must introduce self-remembering to each event in one's life, regardless of how commonplace it seems. And truly, the many common events of one's day have their own endearing charm.

Mr. Ouspensky said that false personality is both attractive and amusing and it will find noble titles for its weaknesses. Attempting to avoid amusing conversation is a large aim to pose for oneself, but one should be willing to discard anything that takes the place of self-remembering. False personality thinks one has to be in a temple or at an isolated retreat in order to produce consciousness. One must pursue self-remembering regardless of one's circumstances, because without it, one does not exist.

David—World 6, higher intellectual center—must slay Goliath—false personality.

False personality is opposed to self-remembering because its illusory life is at stake. False personality craves novelty. It seeks one new thing after another rather than being content with the simplicity of self-remembering. Self-remembering is always an interruption to false personality. Try to ignore the 'I's that don't want to work.

The time we spend away from our meetings tests our being. In your daily life with other students, try not to support false personality in yourself and others by becoming another person. With life, remember to use intentional insincerity and enact false personality.

False personality is influenced by other people's 'I's because it is under feminine dominance and wants to be liked. Eventually, one will be externally considerate of the needs of others without becoming concerned with fulfilling their expectations.

False personality tries to occupy the present in place of higher centers. We should value most the subject that false personality values least: self-remembering. Being discontented with self-remembering is a major condition for false personality. The system is as simple as one can imagine, and false personality will undermine it by making it seem complicated. Despite the cosmology, the bottom line is to be where you are.

Students are often taken in by their false personality asking questions, including questions about esoteric ideas. I have stressed that the answer is a state, not a question. Don't be fooled by false personality's curiosity. That, too, can undermine self-remembering. The knowledge of the system is brilliant, but it can also deceive one if one becomes preoccupied with it.

False personality has no concept of unity; there is no honor among thieves. The 'I's of false personality can mount an attack, but they can't sustain it against true personality when one has entered the way.

Impatience is so much easier than self-remembering or transforming negative emotions. It is a real deception, a buffer. It is nonsense to become negative with someone and then to chastise oneself for doing so. It's a waste of time, and time is almost all we have. It is difficult for a teacher to keep students from making small problems into large problems because to false personality, the bigger the problem, the more important one is.

It is common for awakening to be destructive at first because one must remove false personality in order to prepare the foundation for true personality. Mr. Ouspensky commented that this system is not popular because one is asked to relinquish mechanical attitudes, beliefs and manifestations. He added that, even so, one has nothing to lose. The process of destruction is healthy if it is followed by the process of construction. Essence is dear and does not wish awakening to be a severe process, yet it is a severe process, whether one experiences the way of denial or the way of love.

False personality is a compilation of unconscious acts acquired from others, but essence is intrinsic to one, is one's own. Essence in its undeveloped state is severely limited because it cannot divide its attention. True personality is designed to develop essence.

The real part of us is strong. Of course, the other part—false personality—does not exist at all; it is all lies, all imitation, all borrowed, and it complicates matters by thinking that its acts are all original, all its own.

When you make difficult observations about your mechanicality, you must not identify and start a chain of negativity. You must reaffirm your aim to remember yourself.

False personality doesn't see itself as false; it feels it has the right answer for every situation.

False personality, with its numerous masks, occupies the space of true personality and self-remembering. It's a relief to begin to form true personality. One can see that one's false personality happened to one but, with self-remembering, one begins to fill one's centers profitably and to mold oneself.

In the Fourth Way it is necessary to practice intentional insincerity, which is designed to minimize the negativity directed at one by life people. Yet it is a difficult performance to enact when one is in essence and another person is in false personality. To be successful one would need to remember oneself. There is no situation that cannot serve one as an opportunity for self-remembering.

The appearance of higher centers and essence is the result of an accumulated effort. The absence of essence is caused by a lack of effort. We each waste opportunities because the areas of friction that higher forces select are considered too sacred by false personality. If friction were not given where identification exists, one would remain a machine.

You have to examine what takes the place of self-remembering, and experience an internal civil war.

Self-remembering is not dependent upon body type, center of gravity, alchemy or chief feature, because consciousness is not functions. When higher centers do appear, false personality will question them since its existence is threatened by their birth. One's self is a new being—a new man.

We are critical of others because we are disappointed with ourselves. One pitiful dimension of false personality is that in addition to reducing oneself, it tries to reduce others. It is a law that the lower will try to consume the higher.

Laughter abounds with false personality and infra-sex, which is why laughter is often unappealing. Sometimes we laugh when we enter and exit a room, as this buffer helps the machine establish its position in the environment.

Often our machines will smile under pressure when there is no reason to smile. This pseudo-emotion is a buffer and originates in false personality. Smiling and laughing are often a dimension of false personality, but this doesn't mean that smiles and laughter are harmful to one's evolution, because essence is cheerful.

We live in a huge galaxy. People look beyond the earth to the galaxy, forgetting they are standing on a small planet. This galaxy, of which we are a part, is an insignificant part of the universe. We occasionally ask the naïve question, "Are we influenced by these enormous heavenly bodies?" False personality may not allow us to lift our heads to the sky because this reveals the minute scale of human existence.

The biggest weakness of false personality is that it lacks unity. It does not have self-remembering.

Some students lose time because they stay in the same relationship to an idea by associating with people who strengthen their false personalities.

One has nothing but the present. False personality thrives on chaos. There is usually no fire; people may scream fire, but there is no fire. One must isolate oneself from various impostors.

Duality is obviously designed into our machines. We have two eyes, two ears, two arms, two hands, two legs, two feet and two nostrils. If one studies physiognomy, one can see two different people in one machine because the left side of the body, essence, is a different being from the right side. A person's right eye harbors personality, the left eye is where his essence resides.

Essence is naïve and expects kindness from life, so one should quickly shield essence with true personality if one encounters negativity. One can remember that other people are machines to the extent one realizes that, without self-remembering, one is also mechanical.

The result of remembering oneself is the penetration of essence. One progresses from World 48 to World 24, eventually entering Worlds 12 and 6. Essence is quiet and timid, soft and gentle, while false personality is obvious and loud.

One limitation of essence is that it will become fascinated with what it observes. One needs to practice divided attention so that one's essence can be transformed into higher centers.

Essence has its limitations. For the Martial type, the expression of negative emotions is a weakness inherent in essence, just as dominance is for the Saturnine type. A feature is incapable of viewing itself as a limitation, so it seems harmless to the machine. This attitude results from subjective thinking. The Martial type, therefore, must learn to be repelled by negative emotions.

Initially, one's center of gravity is a major denying force. Then, as one studies the system and tries to be the words, one begins to use one's center of gravity in order to awaken, by transforming its limitations and developing its positive qualities. One's work must become emotional, and all who enter the way become emotional by penetrating essence, which is independent of one's center of gravity.

What displaces negative emotions is essence, and essence is the bridge to higher centers.

All types are attractive when they are in essence.

If essence is aware both of itself and of the object viewed, higher centers are functioning. If a sternness accompanies that energy, however, one's instinctive center is probably feigning higher centers.

Essence has no value unless it is accompanied by divided attention. It basically ornaments the earth and is, in a sense, used by the Ray of Creation.

Rilke said, "Never imagine wisdom to be more than the understanding of a child." Unless one is like a child—in a state of essence—one will not experience one's self.

Why do we wish to concentrate on a talent we have instead of on consciousness?
If you could put the same effort into trying to be conscious, what would you achieve? Even so, we do wish to develop talents within our essence, parallel with self-remembering.

Essence is very simple; we are very simple. It is tragic that one stands in one's own way through one's own 'I's.

By resisting the inclinations of your machine, your true self will emerge.

Many people use their entire lives to strengthen their features rather than their essence.

We need essence in order to experience higher centers. It takes a number of years, in reality lifetimes, to transform essence into higher centers.

Buffers and
The Many 'I's

Almost everything is a buffer to self-remembering. It's much easier to be in imagination, to be identified or to be negative than to self-remember. They are all convenient substitutes. Since self-remembering is not mechanical, it is very difficult. *Anything* is a deviation if one is not self-remembering.

When we blame an event or another person for our negativity we are buffering; we still haven't gotten to the bottom of things as long as we are blaming someone else. We buffer our inability to remember ourselves by blaming others. Neither are we ourselves to blame. That, too, is not self-remembering.

Buffers are often active when self-remembering is absent. However, we can function without buffers—they are unnecessary when self-remembering is present. Buffering is not a permanent condition. One's machine may buffer for a few seconds and then, through divided attention, a higher state may arrive. We strengthen the desire to awaken by removing buffers and illusions, although this process takes time. As the years pass, we understand more profoundly that everything is barren without self-remembering.

The many 'I's buffer the simplicity of self-remembering. The intellectual center can pose questions indefinitely, distracting one from self-remembering. We should try to see many of these questions as buffers. To ask why shocks occur has its place, but the question is insignificant compared to transforming shocks into self-remembering and gripping the present.

Unnecessary suffering buffers one's inability to remember oneself. Being dissatisfied is also a buffer to self-remembering, but what is not? Unlike people without the system, we replace buffers with self-remembering.

How can we avoid trying to compete with others in the work?
By realizing that competition is a buffer to self-remembering, that we aren't running a race with one another; we are here to help one another through second line work. The 'I's that are overly concerned with one's pace in the school are an expression of vanity.

Self-pity is a buffer to self-remembering; any negative emotion is a buffer to self-remembering. It is much easier to be negative than to be present. Why not replace self-deprecation with self-remembering? It is difficult to displace buffers because one must replace them with self-remembering, and yet nothing is more real or more satisfying.

How do you feel when you see your students becoming identified with the form of the school?
It is a buffer to being present, but nearly everything is. Influence C takes appropriate measures to minimize identification.

What replaces self-remembering is a variety of unimportant phenomena, such as negative emotions, imagination, identification and other features. Imagination and the expression of negative emotions use one's sex energy if self-remembering doesn't. Imagination and the expression of negative emotions are the major forces that hinder self-remembering. If one can control these two negative forces, essence will displace them. Essence is one's own—unlike false personality, it is not an imitation of something. To the extent one deviates from the present, one is in false personality.

We should struggle to prevent self-remembering from disappearing behind our daily petty emotions. For instance, if we have misplaced a pen, we should not have our emotional life determined by this. It is only a pen, and we have something within us that can become immortal through not identifying with events large or small.

Impatience, like all negative emotions, is a substitute for self-remembering. Eventually, we realize that negative emotions are designed to buffer our inability to remember ourselves. There are so many negative emotions one can indulge in, each attempting to occupy the space reserved for one's self. In the fairy tale, Snow White (higher emotional center, or World 12) was warned not to trust the witch, who would return in a variety of different costumes. In the same way, the queen of hearts will entice one with various subjects with which to identify.

One needs to study other people, as well as oneself, to understand how features such as tramp, vanity or fear manifest. One must realize, however, that one cannot observe these things without remembering oneself. When one evaluates one's work, it is necessary to avoid the negative emotion of disappointment. One must understand that one gains something real and eternal when one self-remembers, regardless of how small that gain may appear to be.

Recently there was a large earthquake. Will there be larger earthquakes soon?
A cataclysmic disaster may be imminent that could be a prelude to hydrogen warfare. If California fell, there would be no major population center near Apollo and so the coast would be clear. Plato said: "War is a permanent state for humanity." Humanity will always suffer war and upheavals; we are fortunate that we don't have to wait for an earthquake to divide our attention. From one angle, it makes no difference what occurs—earthquakes, warfare or something else. We still can't afford to use

time carelessly. All we can do is remember ourselves before, during and after an event occurs. We can't wait for predictions or prophesies to come true or to fail, because then we would remember ourselves only two or three times in our lives. Shocks are material for evolution, and rising above them is a must for us. Denying force, large or small, is always an opportunity.

Higher forces arrange that some events which we anticipate do not arrive so that we can learn to be wary of anticipation 'I's. Higher forces slowly corner one into the living present by gradually removing a series of lies.

Death is in the cards for the physical body, but we can become immortal. Surviving one's own many 'I's, penetrating the present; that is the final battleground.

Mr. Ouspensky made so many great statements. One of them was that consciousness is not mind activity. Our higher centers are none of the many 'I's, thank goodness!

Pinocchio became a real boy—World 6—and eventually prevailed over the fox and the cat (instinctive-moving and emotional centers).

It is not the event, the person, or the time of life that is the obstacle, it is one's own many 'I's.

Think of the great chaos that exists each day within us. We have random minds that move associatively from one area to another, and we call that "man." It is a generous title for a divine comedy.

The many 'I's are quite difficult, aren't they? They appear, uninvited. One must try not to take them for one's self, because they are not one's self. Isn't it interesting how there are so many different characters in one's being? Different parts of centers ascend and produce 'I's from their respective functions. One's mind is like the weather—unpredictable. The many 'I's are quite taken with themselves, and all of the 'I's use the same speaker. It is curious how the many 'I's dance across our minds and we select the one we wish to express. Don't become preoccupied with them; rather, with self-remembering.

Every day is a struggle to retrieve the present from imagination. The many 'I's don't have unity, but our steward has the concept of unity. So, between the upheavals and during them, we make progress. We all have many 'I's in the intellectual center that invite us to leave the present. One has to scurry back to the present throughout one's life.

The many 'I's lead one around. It's difficult to unglue oneself from them—somehow one has to keep one's distance during active and inactive times. One has to wait until one has found an 'I' that is acceptable to work with. Few thoughts are useful, and thirty or forty useless thoughts can occur internally before a productive one emerges.

One cannot let down for a second because features or the many 'I's will replace self-remembering. It's amazing what floats around in our minds. One must develop an 'I' in one's steward that cautions one to avoid being entertained by one's own 'I's. Some 'I's are innocuous, yet they still exist at the expense of self-remembering. Furthermore, false personality is so clever that certain devious 'I's will attempt to undermine one's work by pursuing what seem to be harmless, entrancing subjects.

The more one awakens, the more bizarre are the 'I's that Influence C gives one; they jolt the ruling faculty, producing higher centers. We all go through periods of extreme behavior, and during these times our work is to remember ourselves and persevere. At some point, we have to exhaust the spectrum of the emotional center. The emotional center tries to destroy self-remembering whenever it can, even under the most pleasant circumstances. If it is morning, it wants to think about the afternoon.

The many 'I's are irrelevant. They are, from one angle, like ants crawling through the brain. To identify with them is even worse. The 'I's can be treacherous, so at times one must trust no 'I', just be present. Any 'I' is strange that is not related to self-remembering. We turn lead into gold when we transform the many 'I's into self-remembering. William Blake said: "The eagle never lost so much time as when he submitted to learn of the crow."

One cannot change one's level of being unless one works beyond one's present abilities. In such instances, as Epictetus said, "Now is the trial for Mount Olympus." The machine has many manifestations that take the place of self-remembering. But these are just words, and each of you must understand this for yourself. You have to learn not to be fooled by your machine and the ways it tries to undermine your work. Each of our machines is driven to undermine self-remembering in some way because it cannot be present.

One must learn to be content with the present. Marcus Aurelius said: "When the ruling faculty is discontented with anything that happens, then it deserts its post."

After many years working with the system and Influence C, no matter what the 'I's say, I have learned not to believe them, and to let them pass. One always looks for new 'I's that would undermine one's work; one does not become careless. When you verify that the machine is not real, you will be propelled to remember yourself.

When Rodney Collin met Mr. Ouspensky, some students had been studying with Mr. Ouspensky for fifteen years. Yet he surpassed them and became fully conscious, because of his fate and his sincere desire to pursue awakening rather than the deviations that obstruct awakening. Although there is nothing for the machine in self-remembering, how great our thinking is when we pursue divided attention rather than the myriad deviations that the machine offers. Everything is a pathetic alternative to being present.

IMAGINATION
AND IDENTIFICATION

It is useful to think about what interfered with self-remembering today. One can observe that many of the situations that brought sorrow or joy were not worthy of those states, because their scale was small. If one is waiting to be served food, one should control the negative emotion of annoyance. And when the food arrives, one should control the positive emotion of joy. Both are equally mechanical and exist on a restricted plane.

In my long history of working with this system, one of the strangest observations has been that one has to be taught to remember oneself—it seems so obvious. One can understand forgetting a coat or umbrella, but to forget one's self is unpardonable. William Shakespeare said, "Men are men and the best sometimes forget." Even Christ forgot himself at times. When he went to sleep in the boat and the waters became troubled, he was awakened to calm the storm. Esoterically, the boat was the school and the waters were truth; the truth was being distorted.

When one is not remembering oneself one is under the law of accident. How often does one remember oneself throughout the day? It's like being in a boat without a rudder—self-remembering is the rudder that keeps us on course. Becoming negative about being controlled by the law of accident is as mechanical as the law of accident itself. One has to be careful when one is intrigued by lateral octaves that divert one from the main octave of remembering oneself.

The hidden purpose of rarely using the word 'I' in our publications is to discourage people from taking themselves too seriously and thinking about themselves too much. Higher centers simply cannot break through excessive self-indulgence. It shuts one off from higher centers, and it is its own punishment. Try to remember that negative states don't last, and in two or three days they will be surpassed by higher ones.

Laughter commonly follows accidents and is a buffer that promotes identification. Self-remembering and laughter rarely appear together. Laughter is more often connected with infra-sex, although it has its place. It can help relieve tension, and is a way that the machine releases superfluous energy.

The identification with one's inability to remember oneself is a difficult negative emotion to surmount. Yet a properly developed steward will prevent such subtle negativity from hindering one's further efforts to awaken.

When one begins to awaken the question naturally arises as to how one can become more emotional without becoming identified, because when we identify, we lose our identity. In order to become more emotional, one must strengthen an immature emotional center by appreciating self-remembering rather than identifying with the subject at hand. One can also become more emotional by controlling artificial emotions that appear through unconscious acting.

Identification is generally allowed to exist because it buffers the inability to remember oneself. One's machine will identify over small and large matters with equal intensity, so desperate is it to undermine self-remembering.

It is startling to awaken and discover that one has identified with something trivial. One's work is swept away when one becomes identified. Struggling against identification is hard, but it wouldn't be worth anything if it weren't difficult.

Imagination is the natural state of man. Negative emotions are more subject to control than imagination is. One needs to understand that one's problems are *maya,* or illusion. One identifies with relatively unimportant phenomena, such as one's children, one's wife, one's husband, or one's home. When one awakens, one sees that these aspects of one's life are to be respected, and yet they are not real. Although they can enhance one's evolution, they can also hinder it if one identifies with them.

Our major problem is how to avoid identifying with problems. One's own identity will eventually displace identification. For identification, we give up our greatest treasure, self-remembering.

I was speaking with a student today who was trying to convince me that my job is unbearable. I said, "No, I enjoy my job as a teacher. It can only become unbearable if I identify with it." One has to watch as carefully as one can and try not to identify, which requires self-remembering. I often ask myself: "Do you wish to sacrifice self-remembering for the present identification?"

Identification, regardless of the subject, is a negative emotion and thwarts self-remembering. The subject of identification is not important; zero times zero is still zero.

Try not to identify when you observe your machine lying, because all machines are subject to this manifestation. Lying permeates all four centers, as each has its own set of lies. If one wishes to stop lying, one must pose the aim to control centers. To control centers, one must return to remembering oneself, since nothing can be done in sleep. It doesn't matter what one's machine is doing if one is asleep. Our bodies were designed to sleep, not to awaken, so we must go against nature.

Identification masquerades as humility: frequently what one takes for humility is identifying with one's imaginary picture of oneself.

If you aren't careful you will spend a large part of your life in identification. We have to recognize identification for what it is, and then step back. There is absolutely nothing in it. Some of the things we take seriously you couldn't sell for a penny.

People want symbols of identity because they don't have identity itself.

One cannot sever old bonds without pain but, at any time, oneself or another may cease to grow; this is truly death.

I was working with a little identification today and I realized that identification takes our time, and time is all we have.

Consciousness has degrees, and identification is truly a state of madness. Very small things catch us. When we are not identified we see identification for what it is—a waste of time. Sometimes Influence C sets back an octave to remind us why we're here—to not identify.

The best way to help another person who is identified is to not become identified oneself. When two people are identified, their chances of self-remembering are further diminished. When another person is experiencing true grief, the best approach is to not identify; even though certain identifications are difficult, they represent an exceptional opportunity to grow. One must attempt to control negative emotions, regardless of how justified they appear to be. One must remember that a higher right exists—the right to be one's self.

One has difficulties with others because one has difficulties with oneself.

How can we develop will without introducing identification into our efforts?
Identification, regardless of the subject, is a negative emotion. Certain capacities are unattainable if sought too zealously. Thus, one cannot receive one's self by being preoccupied with oneself. Witnessing real results can bring emotionality to one's work, for one's self appears when one transcends identification. Many ideas of the system can only be understood if one has had a legitimate experience with higher centers.

It is not possible to evolve without confronting one's deepest identifications.

What is the largest denying force to self-remembering?
Imagination, which is the natural state of man. One may forget that the events of imagination never took place. It is a state we will have to struggle with throughout our lives.

Imagination is as harmful a manifestation as the expression of negative emotions and, although the machine appears more tranquil in imagination, one is still not awake. We must keep trying to break through the clouds of imagination. Omar Khayyam said, "There was the Door to which I found no Key: there was the veil through which I could not see." The veil is imagination, and the key is self-remembering. We lift the veil by self-remembering. Imagination is one of the final barriers between oneself and higher centers.

Imagination consumes energy and intrudes into all circumstances so that reality can seem to be a foreign experience. When you yield to imagination, something great disappears behind something small. Self-remembering is quite accessible and can penetrate any moment of your day. It may commence at any time and may interrupt any negative emotion. Imagination is more prevalent than chief feature—it is our greatest foe.

It's interesting to sit in this room this evening and think of sitting in this room in thirty years. The struggle will be the same—to be present, taste the wine and listen to the music. Imagination will be a curse for the rest of our lives. Some forms of negative imagination are less offensive than others, and false personality will even consider them pleasant. When we understand sincerely that imagination is not self-remembering, we begin to successfully separate from it. Every second of self-remembering penetrates imagination and pierces eternity.

One can see how desperate our condition is when one discovers oneself in imagination while the topic of self-remembering is being discussed. One can remember oneself but, to do so, one must desire to awaken.

How can we work with sexual imagination?
All imagination, regardless of the subject, exists on the same plane. One must struggle just as much with other forms of imagination as with sexual. If that subject remains difficult for a long period of time, one should consider marriage.

False personality does not wish its false life of imagination interrupted by the reality of self-remembering.

Formatory mind is strong in us. When we are actually in the third state, the machine will look for words to describe that state. When we experience higher centers, we have to guard them quite carefully because of the machine's wish to interrupt them. It will try a variety of methods to put the self back to sleep. At a certain stage of development, a useful 'I' to protect a higher experience is, "Trust no 'I's—be present now."

William Shakespeare said, "For all the day our eyes view things unrespected." Often we are not present to the simple beauty inherent in our environment because imagination vies with the present for our attention. The present takes us everywhere; imagination, nowhere. Imagination uses the energy that belongs to higher centers. There are many practical ways to intercept imagination, and these methods do not diminish the mystical aspects of awakening. The more practical the school, the more mystical the school. In order to interrupt imagination, one must be remembering oneself.

How beautiful it is when self-remembering glows in the darkness of imagination. Imagination is like night, and self-remembering is day.

Isn't it odd that we have to be taught to live in the present? When one awakens to discover the machine speaking, a sense of alarm courses through one because one realizes that one's machine functions adequately in sleep.

How can one learn to be more compassionate toward other students? Remember Influence C is helping all who enter the way and we help both ourselves and Influence C through external consideration. We are considerate of one another, which allows us to share the experience of essence. We must also forgive one another and ourselves for our mistakes. We are here because we are imperfect. If one is not being sincere with people in the school, one is not remembering oneself, and injures oneself as much as others. One must recommence self-remembering many times each day. One loses the thread, finds it, loses it again and one must find it again. One awakens, puzzled as to what one has said or done, for asleep, one simply cannot know.

When you are confused, try to apply common sense to your actions: listen to the music, read the book, work with the task at hand. It is possible to apply a few great principles throughout your lifetime that can ensure your evolution, such as attempting to remember yourself, to resist expression of negative emotions, and to avoid identification. Identification is frequently responsible for confusion. You learn to avoid identifications by not attaching yourself to them.

It is a terrible battle we fight with imagination and imaginary denying force—it is just ridiculous. One cannot transform imaginary suffering; one only gets imaginary results. One can transform real suffering and produce an immortal astral body.

FRICTION

The subject we return to each time we meet is self-remembering and what prevents it. Two familiar adversaries of self-remembering are imagination and identification. They will haunt one throughout one's life and occupy the space that should be reserved for one's self. Although the subject of identification varies, one's machine persistently reasons that if certain problems were resolved, one's friction would be eliminated. One cannot evolve, however, without transforming friction.

One of the best things about friction is that it passes, and we prevail. Goethe said, "Continue, because you must." There must be tension in one's machine to awaken, but most people are asleep, and do not produce enough tension to transform and thus to awaken.

When friction is intense and it is difficult to control internal storms, one must use common sense. Mr. Ouspensky said that in certain instances, when one cannot remember oneself, one can only make the attempt. When friction becomes extreme we may succumb or become indifferent. Mr. Ouspensky said, "If friction stops, self-remembering stops." Under real stress all philosophical wisdom gives way to the silent bearing of the ruling faculty.

When friction is intense we may forget that it is a play; when it subsides, we realize the shock was intended to reveal identification and develop higher centers. There is no escaping suffering, with or without the school. If one is brave, one prays for more assistance. We have been given hearts that can endure great suffering.

Sometimes one cannot remove oneself from the negativity one is experiencing. Control, however, begins with observation. Rodney Collin suggested that when one is identified and under great stress, one should try to remember that a higher alternative is available to one—self-remembering. When a man number four transforms suffering, he is performing the work of an incomplete man number five.

One of the ways Influence C works is by arranging friction or trials that we are intended to transform. They bring terrifying friction for us to transform into an astral body through self-remembering.

How can one attract the friction necessary to be more awake?
Introduce inconspicuous voluntary suffering into your life. Artificial pressures are helpful for remembering oneself. Find ways to make more effort; don't waste time.

One needs to be shocked to the point that shocks don't touch one. One is fortunate to receive friction in the form of small, or large, shocks. If Influence C provides a shock while one is trying to be present, it is a third force that catapults one into the third state of consciousness. Influence C creates many shocks to keep one off balance. Fortunately, we can use small shocks as well as large ones to evolve. We also need to take the initiative by using—with moderation—many forms of inconspicuous voluntary suffering. Be creative in a positive way.

A student spoke to me about being in an interval in self-remembering, and I was taken aback, because it is always a second-to-second struggle. Jesus said, "The son of man [World 6] hath not where to lay his head."

Influence C does not give you friction because you are bad, but because you are asleep. One's essence misunderstands this because of feminine dominance, and has a tendency to enter self-pity rather than self-remembering.

What do you think is the greatest friction?
Imagination and identification. Awakening is a second-to-second struggle, moment to moment, hour to hour. We know we have today, and we may not even have the rest of this day.

It has been an unusually difficult time for people. One student fell twelve feet off a scaffold. Another fell from a ladder and has his neck in a brace. Two students had a fire at their home. Another student is going through depositions in a lawsuit. Two other students just found out their mothers have terminal cancer. Influence C is giving friction so we can come together emotionally for the vineyard harvest. Don't wait for the friction to end. Try to avoid the attitude, "When will this end?" Rilke wrote: "How dear you are to me, you nights of sorrow. Why do I not kneel more to receive you, and give myself more loosely unto you? We, wasters of sorrow. How we gaze beyond them into some drab duration to see if they may not end there."

We are here because it is difficult. If it were easy, none of us would be here.

You receive friction when you need it. The lovely thing about trials is that they force real students to surface, and force the ones who aren't real out of the school. I have so many wonderful friends, and they all need friction to awaken. One has to keep things in perspective. One can't escape without friction, and we have been instructed in how to transform suffering. One's mechanical morality thinks friction is punishment, but Influence C gives us suffering not as punishment, but to transform into an astral body and a soul.

The aim is not to suffer; everyone suffers. The aim is to transform suffering into an astral body.

If we self-remember when experiencing friction, we assimilate suffering. It is certain no one will escape friction. One of the purposes of friction is to bring us closer together, and allow us to grow through our trials. There are barriers we go through, or that Influence C pushes us through. It can be a shock to make it through these barriers.

As soon as friction arrives, we want to know how to get rid of it; we can hardly wait for it to be over. It is mechanical to resist friction, but divine to transform it. One can become exasperated under pressure, yet one must try to not allow oneself to reach that point. It inevitably happens. The only way out is to change one's level of being through not identifying.

I cannot think of an older student who is not tottering under the pressure. Because we must work beyond our level of being to change our level of being, periodically our roles prove too difficult for each of us.

Do we all have to wrestle with the same friction?
The subject of denying force is irrelevant. Sometimes denying force excites me, because it is our food. There is a wonderful pressure in the school now. Each person has a little too much to do, but it's healthy to have too much to do.

It is a great time to self-remember when your life is on the line. Homer said, "Submit in silence." The only answer is self-remembering. Everyone gets crunched, but we come through our trials the stronger for them.

Through trials, try to maintain a high standard of self-remembering. Simply enduring friction indicates one has approached the level of a steward.

We can't escape through thinking; we can't escape through laughing or crying; we can only escape through self-remembering.

MAKING EFFORT

Life is asleep, and we are going against the stream. Like salmon with a strong homing instinct, we must swim against the current of life's sleep to remember ourselves and develop our souls. What is it to be a man, but to struggle against the current of the masses, and through great labor and desolate trials create one's soul? One begins with self-remembering in the morning and finishes with it at night. One can never afford to lay self-remembering aside; one ceases to exist.

You cannot awaken unless you have verified that you are asleep.

Sleep is so unappealing that it propels one to awaken. People do not make more efforts to awaken because they do not understand that their time is limited. When one deeply and truly understands that one's time is limited, regardless of one's age, one will strive to awaken with the mass of one's being. Higher forces become more serious with one as each year progresses.

It would be nice to say that the material in this book is behind me. But self-remembering is never behind us. It has no momentum of its own and is always an uphill battle. Leonardo da Vinci said, "Thou, O God, dost sell unto us all good things at the price of labor." We are in an extremely difficult situation. Almost no one realizes the enormity of what can be gained or lost during his lifetime. One gains immortality or suffers oblivion, or worse. Every second you remember yourself you pierce eternity.

No one puts enough pressure on himself to awaken, which is why Influence C provides shocks. It takes more to awaken than one knows, and more than the machine is willing to admit. Psalm 127 says, "Except the Lord build the house, they labor in vain that build it." Esoterically this means that those who do not build on self-remembering build in vain, as in the Bible "Lord" refers to one's own higher centers, and "Lord God" refers to the Absolute. One cannot reap if one has not sown. We are sowing with self-remembering and, at the end of our lives, we will reap what we have sown.

Remember that you are being present for yourself as well as for your school; everything physical will perish; you, with divided attention, will not.

We labor to make the incomprehensible, comprehensible. Self-remembering is a challenge we have to accept even though at times it seems almost too much, seems beyond our capacity, our level of being. We have to do it every day. The answers required to break through to the present are simple; the efforts, however, are difficult. Even so, we are winning.

The poet Rainer Rilke said, "It is tiresome to be full of retrieving." One keeps trying to retrieve self-remembering from imagination, and it is tiring, yet one could not have a more worthwhile battle on one's hands. There are terrible periods of imagination and then the strain of self-remembering returns. In virtually everything we do, so many of our efforts are toward self-remembering and are related to culture. The opportunities to be present remain the same over the years.

One reason we are attracted to self-remembering is because it is so difficult. It's the only real challenge that one has met in one's life and the only thing that is not mechanical. Courage can have limitations, and awakening requires more perseverance than courage. It does come to that—simply enduring—and it is a good place to be.

There is a line from Goethe that reminds me of a man number four pursuing self-remembering, which is so difficult that it sometimes seems like an illusion: "Ye wavering forms draw near again as ever, when ye long since moved past my clouded eyes. To hold you fast, shall I this time endeavor? Still does my heart that strange illusion prize?"

After having spent the day working for the school, trying to be present, not expressing negativity and trying to avoid imagination, one becomes weary, and yet it is a day well spent. There can be no gain in abandoning the work. The plain truth is that there is no alternative to making efforts to be present, daily, for the rest of one's life.

Students who enter the way work at a full pace. Never lay self-remembering aside. Consciousness cannot be given, it must be earned through one's own efforts, aided by higher forces.

Keep using common sense, and try to take your mind off yourself. Read, take a walk, look after someone else. Avoid over self-indulgence. Influence C does reckless things to produce a process of elimination with people in the school. I don't resist this, I am all for it. It cleans the school.

In trying to awaken, one has to realize that there are no guarantees. Goethe, one of the most intelligent conscious beings, wrote in *Faust*, "To this thought I hold unswerving, to wisdom's final fruit profoundly true: of freedom and of life he only is deserving, who every day doth master them anew." If you want to be immortal, you will get it; if you want something else you will get it. Most people spend their lives pursuing Influence A rather than Influence C.

Mr. Ouspensky stressed the necessity of controlling our functions. And yet, in the dismal situations in which we find ourselves, we are apt to be almost out of control. How did we come to have the control that we have? Through effort and time and separating from suffering.

What does it mean to make extra efforts?
Cicero said, "There is not a moment without some duty." If nothing else, we always have the duty to self-remember. Our work can only be serious in proportion to our understanding of the depth of our sleep. The teacher can only communicate *knowledge,* the teacher cannot communicate *being*—it is your own responsibility to be the words.

Sometimes I speak as if I know, but I am speaking for myself. I do not expect anything to be either believed as true, or rejected as false, but taken neutrally as theory and verified. Still, I know what I know. So many concepts that students struggle with are facts for me: body type, center of gravity, chief feature, alchemy. But until they are facts for you, you have to struggle. One must work beyond one's capacities daily to change one's level of being. This is a law. We are capable of much more effort, and Influence C must use their time to squeeze that out of us.

You can't retire from self-remembering. A seventy-year-old student must make the same effort to produce higher centers as one who is twenty.

One must never be content to go at the pace of anyone else. The last words of Peter Ouspensky were, "Aim, aim; more effort, more effort." Then his physical body died and his astral body was released. Aim to remember yourself and place more effort into remembering yourself. It takes more effort to awaken than we realize. Shocks help wring this understanding out of us.

The main principle that guides your life is self-remembering. Efforts based upon identification diminish as you begin to awaken. Self-remembering must be a perpetual struggle and is the dearest of all labors, since nothing of value is attained without effort. You must transform suffering to appreciate the great simplicities of life.

One way to avoid using words for registering impressions is to employ the looking exercise. It is not uncommon to experience a different thought with each heartbeat. If one shifts one's head slightly every three seconds to receive a new impression, one can sever the 'I's that wish to respond to the objects one is viewing. While walking one can also concentrate one's attention on an object that is within reasonable distance, and try not to allow thoughts to manifest until one has passed that impression. These exercises can serve to usher you into the present.

How can one use the realization that a long time has elapsed since one last thought of trying to self-remember?
When you become disappointed at the lack of self-remembering, immediately try to remember yourself. Use this observation as a catalyst for making more effort; somehow, increase desire. Also, remember not to become negative because Influence C will jar you from your sleep; be sure to choose self-remembering over self-pity.

Our task is great, greater than anyone knows. It is to remember ourselves daily, in both commonplace and trying situations until our last breath. One must endeavor to remember oneself in the most humble circumstances because self-remembering has no momentum of its own. Mr. Ouspensky said that a man number five can be present when he needs to be, but even that is a lot of work. When I listen to a concert, for example, I feel there is as much responsibility on me to hear every note as there is on the artist to play those notes.

When 'I's circulate that wish immediate results for one's efforts, one can be assured that one is not remembering oneself. These 'I's can serve, however, as a useful shock to help one remember oneself. Negative states initially appear to be a curse, but later become a blessing as one begins to transform the negativity. Fortunately, self-remembering begets self-remembering, and is its own reward.

How can we act consistently?
If one could act consistently, one would be acting consciously, because one would have unity and not be a different person in different environments. As one studies people, one will see different groups of 'I's in them that are subject to changing circumstances. One should expect something reliable from people in a school since they are trying to be unified. Consistency is based upon remembering oneself. To act consistently requires unity; to be unified requires self-remembering. To remember yourself you must have the aim to be present.

One must observe whether one experiences the same personality, and makes the same efforts privately, as one does publicly. And if one does behave differently publicly, efforts are founded on vanity or feminine dominance.

How can we be more in the present when our machine wishes to plan for future needs?
To everything there is a season. There is a place to plan for future needs, which is common sense. Don't prolong the process, and once it is finished, focus on the present. While planning, use inconspicuous voluntary suffering by holding the paper at a slightly odd angle, sitting a little too close to the desk, and so on.

The 'I', "This is not a permanent state," is the beginning of the end of negative emotions.

I experienced a little difficulty hearing the music tonight. A work 'I' advised me, "You cannot speak if you cannot listen," in a gentle, non-judgmental tone of voice. It was a third force for helping me to listen. Work 'I's are precious, and it is a blessing when they appear when we need them; unfortunately for a man number four the right work 'I' often comes along when the internal battle is over.

It is a big effort to use small opportunities to remember ourselves, and a good part of our lifetime struggle is dedicated to growing up. We are people who are drinking deeply, who have a total commitment to awaken because without it, we could not expect a total reward. The most beautiful achievements are within the reach of all people, but because of man's own neglect they are seldom attained. When we establish an aim and then neglect it, we later awaken and re-establish a connection with the elusive thread of consciousness.

It is important not to cram one's life with events, but to do well whatever one does. One should enjoy reading a book and not just try to get through it. Never allow yourself to be so busy, to be in such a hurry that you forget your precious self.

How can we include the element of surrender in our moment-to-moment effort to self-remember?
We must understand deeply that we have nothing at all to surrender; we give up nothing for something.

Never stop making efforts; remember your aim tenaciously. We change without pressing, and efforts made in one direction can bring gratifying results in another. We do not need external events to urge us to remember ourselves. Self-remembering has a cumulative effect, and the more you remember yourself, the more you will be able to remember yourself.

It is fruitful to work with people who don't have to be convinced of the necessity of remembering themselves. Students get into trouble because they think they can coast. It may surprise one to realize that one must work to awaken. Awakening does not happen

to one. Many people never pass beyond allurement, and they leave
a teaching when they actually have to begin daily work.

We push ourselves to the limit. Keep returning to self-remembering, keep trying to retrieve it—it is the only thing worth pursuing.

Why is it harder to do the work the farther you go?
Because you aren't taken in by imagination, by your imaginary
picture of yourself. We stop being satisfied with imagination and
have stopped fooling ourselves about our condition.

From the realization that man is a machine, the real work starts;
the moment one verifies one is a machine, one starts to cease to
be mechanical.

In the end, people have what it takes to continue, or they don't,
and it is a rough road, but the only one worth traveling.

SUFFERING

One is more apt to be remembering oneself if one is trying to separate from suffering. This is not pleasant information, and it is one of the primary reasons for the system's lack of popularity. Suffering is useless without self-remembering because it is not suffering we seek, but the transformation of suffering.

We have a wrong attitude toward suffering. We think suffering is useless, and we don't know how to use it properly. When situations are difficult, one becomes negative, but one must remember oneself in order to transform suffering. Our machines think words will dispel suffering, but no words can relieve one of some types of friction. Only acceptance can minimize severe suffering.

Unnecessary suffering stems from a lazy mind; it's much easier to suffer unnecessarily than to remember oneself.

There is little reason for some students to receive substantial shocks, because they mistake small suffering for large suffering. They would not know how to separate from a large shock. This is related to our machines' tendency to magnify and exaggerate our suffering.

As one witnesses the months and years pass, one realizes that one's greatest suffering is, ironically, one's *unnecessary* suffering. One is susceptible to unnecessary suffering because it is so difficult to remember oneself. By creating turmoil, or imaginary problems, one takes many events seriously that in no way warrant concern. Shakespeare said: "He jests at scars that never felt a wound." If a man releases his unnecessary suffering, he sees that his pursuits are hollow and that he does not exist. One must fill this void with self-remembering.

Unnecessary suffering is responsible for most unhappiness. Fear and resentment can extend one or two minutes of suffering into hours. Often what stands between you and self-remembering is unnecessary suffering. You must form the habit of opposing fear with self-remembering. When alarm begins to circulate within you because you cannot remember yourself, this, in turn, is material for remembering yourself.

Real grief is not a negative emotion, when there is restraint and silence.

Mr. Gurdjieff said one must use voluntary suffering to awaken. One thing I have used for many years now is to keep my feet under the table flat and together. I don't turn or roll them from side to side. When I find them in the wrong place it sends a message to me to come to the present. Voluntary suffering should be inconspicuous—other people should not know one is doing it. You can try not drinking tea or coffee for a week, not having vegetables or meat—keep irritating the machine. Your soul is the pearl of great price and, like any pearl, it must be created by transforming irritation. When driving a car by yourself, sit to the right or left or far back on the seat, or sit on a cassette. Play a station you don't like; play it loudly. Do not defeat your will—use voluntary suffering for fifteen minutes and then find something else. There is a way out but you have to be creative to find it.

How can we increase voluntary suffering?
Do what the machine does not want to do, or give the machine what it does not like. When the machine doesn't have big suffering to work with, little suffering will do.

Is voluntary suffering an artificial pressure, or is it legitimate?
It is both artificial and legitimate; it is an artificial pressure that produces a real result.

Voluntary suffering contains an element of will, and yet such efforts should constitute only a fragment of one's day. It may be useful to avoid extreme efforts to suffer voluntarily because false personality will establish impossible aims in order to hinder one's progress and make awakening seem impossible.

Is it easier to self-remember when one is relaxed or tense, than when one is feeling neutral?
All three states are hues of self-remembering and one may find one's self being present when one is relaxed, tense or neutral.

Recently I watched a film about Africa. There were lines of people who had a disease that causes blindness. It didn't seem like things could get worse than that. Not only were they blind, but they were holding sticks, each holding onto the other, following each other, walking to nowhere. There was nowhere to go in that desolate place. It is a complex universe. Why is there the suffering that there is? Perhaps it is the nature of the materials that create suffering. God had to suffer unspeakably to create his astral body, and man was made in the image of God.

One must verify that one does indeed have conscious fate. If this information is correct, it follows that there must be a play written for one in order to actualize this fate, as conscious fate cannot be accidental. The script is real and the suffering is real, for without these elements a real state could not be produced.

Students must learn to separate from a teacher's suffering just as a teacher must separate from his students' trials. Nevertheless, we will continue to be sympathetic to one another. One's self and suffering must often wend a lonely, mystical path, and I make no attempt to conceal the reality that they are melancholy companions. There is, however, light at the end of the tunnel.

One of the most useful 'I's to promote in the midst of friction is, "How can I work with this suffering differently than a person without the system?"

We think we should not experience pain because our mothers, to the best of their abilities, relieved us from suffering. This is a dimension of feminine dominance. We were conditioned to avoid pain and cultivate a biological existence composed of smooth sleep. Awakening is a divine gift, and higher forces use altogether different rules than our mothers. They do, however, love us consciously. The gods are our parents and we are their children and they are making us, like them, immortal. Epictetus said: "I would never desert my true parents, the Gods." Nor would they desert him; indeed, he is one of them now.

We are people who have suffered to find a school, and here we are taught to transform suffering into self-remembering.

We are the fortunate recipients of the work of Influence C, and they have given us the assignment to develop our school. We have received more than our share of understanding here; thus we have also received more than our share of suffering.

Suffering gives us life. Aeschylus said, "It is wisdom's everlasting law that truth can only be learned by suffering it." Transforming suffering requires self-remembering.

There is nothing we can do about suffering except transform it and be present which, after all, is everything. The negative aspects within us produce suffering, which, if transformed, in turn produces higher centers. The best way to work with suffering is to accept it, not ward it off, but let it run its course. Perhaps the most painful aspect of suffering is wishing it to end, because by accepting suffering, one rises above it. Life has many unpleasant moments that one must endure, with or without the system. It takes a long time to learn not to run from suffering, to accept what higher forces give one. Obviously, doubling one's suffering by trying to run away from it is folly.

One's life would be much worse if one did not try to make it better. Through a thousand mistakes, one is born.

Do we bring about our own friction?
Sometimes, through unnecessary suffering. Also, there is an irrevocable play written for each person, and each of us has to pay for receiving our gift of awakening. The most difficult payment is the transformation of suffering.

One cannot transform imaginary suffering into self-remembering; one can only transform real suffering into higher states.

After one has completed a major trial, one realizes with greater understanding that one has lost nothing but illusions. No one can be real without self-remembering, and real suffering consumes imagination.

We lost a student in Mexico City on Monday in an airplane crash. He was sitting at this table on Sunday and his role was complete on Monday. The last statement I made Sunday evening was that young members would give up all they had, as would older students, for self-remembering. Sometimes Influence C asks it of us.

Sadness has its place, but one needs to nip it in the bud and return to self-remembering. William Shakespeare said, "[I] trouble deaf heaven with my bootless cries." The machine will experience self-pity when it receives friction. Although this feature is justifiable on one level, we must refrain from expressing it because of our aim to awaken. To identify is mechanical; to separate is divine. Avoiding self-pity is a great way for us to remember ourselves.

William Blake depicted a warring angel who walked determinedly with a sword by his side. When I first saw this drawing I thought it odd that an angel would bother to be involved in warfare. I now understand that the foe of higher forces is sleep, and that they must use strong measures to awaken us. We receive substantial friction not because of wrong action on our part, but because we are asleep. If one reviews the lives of eminent men, one can observe that their plays are fraught with suffering. Maurice Nicoll said: "Nothing makes a man so like God as suffering."

One's self remembered, through suffering, is the great theme of one's life. One will lose nothing real by sacrificing everything to the moment.

The only way to transform suffering is to accept it. If one accepts it, then one escapes it. Avoiding suffering is suffering itself—it is a great secret.

We know we have no defense save self-remembering when higher forces give us friction. We know we must be silent and accept what they have given us. The truth is quite simple.

How can we remember what we have gained?
One of the things that Influence C accepts about us is that we have to be reminded, that we forget. It's important to try to remember what has been verified, and when it hurts enough we remember.

We each know the suffering we are personally experiencing. This school is real and the shocks have been real. Because we are not pursuing something small, we cannot expect a small payment. There are moments within our lives that cannot be destroyed by time, and transforming suffering accounts for a considerable portion of these moments.

One's attitude toward events, and not events themselves, determines whether or not one will suffer. It is best to conceal one's suffering whenever possible. No words are as touching as silence in the face of suffering. Even in the face of terminal illness, one still has the choice of being present and adding to one's astral body; when death is near and unavoidable, self-remembering reveals itself as everything. At this point one works even more intently on creating a personal tendency to evolve. One's time is counted, and time is nearly all one has.

There must always be friction of sufficient magnitude to produce consciousness. Enduring friction without identification constitutes the greater part of awakening. One does not pass through St. Peter's gates easily.

When one experiences long periods of suffering, there is nothing one can do but endure and transform them. Massive suffering forces one to question the meaning of existence. The greater the suffering, the greater the questioning; remember, there are answers.

Friction is given to all types regardless of their center of gravity. One must pay, with transforming suffering, for the role one is given. Men require formidable suffering to truly make them men, and women must be "as men" and experience enormous friction to awaken. One must become somewhat accustomed to suffering. Friction subsides, yet a more intense form often replaces it. If one persists in trying to transform suffering, one will be less affected by it. Nevertheless, one must experience pain and rise above it.

We have a real life, and we must transform suffering to understand it. One truly understands only what one has suffered. Give yourself this advice: "Suffering is not created for me to identify with, but to transform." To seek relief from suffering through others instead of oneself postpones one's mastery of oneself.

Try to alleviate suffering rather than cause it. When others seem to be losing their work, hold on to your own, and self-remembering will fall into place.

Though we experience beautiful periods, awakening is not intended to be a pleasant process. You must pay the awesome price, and some perceptions are devastating to your cordial nature.

It is necessary to accept suffering as a life-giving principle, and not as an obstacle. There are eminent models from all ways of life—from slaves to emperors—to guide one to a profound existence. Transforming suffering is their common theme.

One can either bend or buckle under pressure. One must stop waiting for it to end and accept it, because the only way to transform suffering is to embrace it.

In Ecclesiastes it is written, "For in much wisdom is much grief, and he that increaseth knowledge increaseth sorrow." Knowledge and being cannot diverge. The knowledge we consume is immortal sustenance designed to produce higher centers. In order to become the words, we must suffer, and yet we must not suffer unnecessarily. We must strive to transform suffering.

We must learn how to use suffering because negative shocks can create the third state. An element within us assumes that suffering will occur to someone else. Yet awakening is not for other people, it is for you. After transforming suffering, one must avoid the tendency to slacken and lapse into sleep.

Transforming and not identifying with suffering opens up all our possibilities. Yet we know that suffering is a sweet and sour experience and is difficult to look forward to. False personality must die within us for higher centers to be born, and we experience that death.

Shocks toll us back to the present and remind us to hold fast to our identity amidst life's temporal folly. We can't expect to awaken without paying the price. There can be no victory without a battle, no virtuous crown without cause. Common sense, however, holds one together. One reason people suffer is because they think of themselves too much; thus they create their own suffering. There are many little secrets to learn in order to awaken, and one of them is that one cannot awaken if one suffers from over self-indulgence. When one learns to reduce excessive self-indulgence and to look about one, higher centers begin to emerge. Higher forces are then assured of having created a compassionate identity—an identity that will serve, rather than selfishly abuse, the Ray of Creation.

Many areas of work may appear insignificant to an uninstructed mind yet, because they can be transformed into something imperishable, they are blessings. We must remember that friction is not what it seems to be. From one angle it can be insidious, but from a higher point of view suffering is a life-giving principle.

The esoteric meaning of wine is understanding. Wine, like understanding, has magical properties and is the color of blood. When Jesus converted water into wine, he transformed truth into understanding, which is a process founded upon suffering. Our suffering makes us a real teaching. The greater the teaching, the greater the suffering and the greater the results. Almost all of Christ's disciples died an unnatural death. We must talk of these things to prepare us for what is to come. Enduring suffering, one takes up one's own cross. We are chosen to play these roles.

One must suffer the same trials to achieve the same spiritual results in any age. Walt Whitman said, "The same inexorable price must still be paid for the same great purchase." This refers to suffering. Each must have the fortune, and the misfortune, to verify that.

No man can know himself without carrying a heart that has endured despair. One must strive for what appears to be inaccessible, for that is where reality dwells, and only despair can scale the greatest walls.

We are all stunned periodically by shocks that draw us into reality. Try not to identify with events that you can't change. Admittedly, receiving shocks is an odd way to escape, but we are fortunate that a way exists at all. Eventually, one accepts shocks not as interruptions in one's life but, thankfully, as interruptions in one's sleep, and values them for bringing forth higher centers.

Let us be touched, but not consumed, by suffering.

Remember, when feelings of helplessness arise, you have help: Influence C. Do not despair; persevere and you shall pierce eternity.

Transformation and Negative Emotions

In the face of suffering, one of our most prevalent weaknesses is resentment. When we receive friction from higher forces, we are intended to transform it rather than identify with it.

Rainer Rilke described man as a "waster of sorrow" because men are apt to resent suffering rather than transform it. Yet, the more one transforms suffering, the more one's soul emerges. It is necessary to remember that a school exists to produce consciousness in its participants. The best way one can serve higher forces is by remembering oneself, because without one's self there is nothing that can serve. It is also necessary to remember why suffering is given, and to try not to become negative. Rilke's statement means that instead of transforming suffering, one enters self-pity and identifies with it.

One of the functions of negative emotions is to distract us from remembering ourselves. Negativity is an unimpressive substitute for the inconspicuous presence of self-remembering. The present eludes one in many ways, and some of these ways, on the surface, can be quite justifiable. Even so, if untransformed, the opportunity to seize the present continues to pass.

How can one prevent self-pity from misusing the work of higher forces? One has to remember that the facts lie, for although the methods utilized by Influence C seem uncivilized, one must attain the higher understanding that transforming suffering creates life. If one assimilates friction correctly, there is no time to indulge in self-pity. Also, self-pity does not prevent Influence C from administering friction, as they are relentless in their aim to awaken you. Self-pity reduces not only oneself, but also others, because it does not wish to be surrounded by success when it is failing.

How can one work on transforming negative energy into positive energy?
Mr. Ouspensky said that the first conscious shock, which is self-remembering, does not occur mechanically, but is a result of one's own efforts. The second conscious shock is produced by one's attempt to transform negative emotions through non-identification. In order to transform negative emotions, one must avoid identifying with the subject of one's negativity. Negative emotions are difficult to transform primarily because one is under feminine dominance and forgets why they are given. One needs to reach for a higher right, which would be to not identify with, and to separate from, negative emotions.

We often experience negative emotions simply because we have accumulated energy in the negative halves of our centers. If one is able to control the initial subject, one will have to be quite alert because the subject of negativity will change. It is the source of negativity that one must eventually control, more than the subject. Mr. Ouspensky said: "We have a worm in us that wishes to express itself."

Plato said we must form good habits. Higher forces provide opportunities to express negative emotions and we must form the habit of not expressing them—then they will turn into true personality, essence and self-remembering. One of the reasons the machine perpetuates negative subjects is because it is easier than resisting them. If a chain of negativity isn't interrupted, it may go on for quite a while.

When life expresses negativity, it is necessary not to let it affect one, but to transform it. One must not transfer life's negativity to students.

Few men who become conscious know their alchemy, center of gravity, chief feature or body type. This knowledge is useful, and yet one's evolution hinges upon the transformation of negative emotions.

Nothing is more noble, nothing is more important, than transforming negative emotions. If you are swamped by a feeling of helplessness, remember that such a state is not permanent, and that you have help within the school and from higher forces. One's wish to awaken increases with each lifetime, as does the intensity of one's friction and the capacity to transform it. Few men have the strength to bear awakening; you are the chosen few.

Something is always trying to distract us from the present—that is often the function of negative emotions. They are a pathetic substitute for self-remembering. We can develop a soul by training ourselves not to express negativity. Mr. Ouspensky said: "No matter what, do not become negative," because one is transforming the si-do shock. The reason that self-remembering is so difficult is that one is simultaneously creating one's soul and awakening one's self. The throes of growth, so to speak. As one transforms suffering, one's aim to awaken grows stronger. How mechanical negative emotions truly are, and how few know the value of transforming suffering.

Nothing but self-remembering can handle negative emotions. Really, it is a question of desire. Mr. Ouspensky rightly said that behind any negative emotion lies one's permission.

One can be self-remembering and still a part of the machine can be negative. When you are beset by negative emotions, remember that the only profitable recourse is to remember yourself.

Negative states are not permanent—that 'I' is the beginning of the end for the negative emotion. Negative emotions lack unity and they do subside. By their nature they are torn and fragmented. We are here because we are imperfect; if we were perfect, unified, we would not be here. Remember to be smart enough to transform negative emotions.

People who are mechanically positive are just as mechanical as people who are mechanically negative. Mr. Ouspensky said: "Some people's false personality functions cheerfully, and thereby they deceive themselves." One cannot control negative emotions if one cannot control positive emotions, and neither is one's self. Self-remembering is metaphysical and is above the transient dualistic plane.

How can one work with losing one's temper?
Anger is a real disappointment when it occurs. It is bad enough we have these 'I's internally, but it is pitiful to express them externally. Mr. Ouspensky said, "You can think anything you wish, but you may not say anything you wish." Each time one expresses a negative emotion toward a fellow student, the school suffers. We try not to wound one another, as the expression of negative emotions in a school is criminal. We have given life to each other to ensure life for each other.

You must transcend the spectrum of the emotional center to create a soul, do more than is humanly possible. Our suffering brings us to the school, but transforming suffering enables us to enter the way. Accepting suffering transforms suffering.

Enduring suffering is a dimension of transforming it. Homer, who encountered additional suffering after his blindness, wrote: "Endure my heart; far worse hast thou endured." When going through small suffering, remember the worst you have gone through.

In reality, the word consciousness is far too generous a title for the first and second states of man's condition. Consciousness has degrees, and bitter negative emotions are more likely to evoke the control of the intellectual parts of centers than are mild negative emotions. Remember that transforming negative emotions is the main method used to awaken, though happily, it is not the only method.

One reaches a point in one's evolution where one is grateful for the terrible 'I's one receives. One sees them as an opportunity for transformation, and is grateful to have one's sleep interrupted. If one cherishes negative emotions, one will be deprived of any joy one might hope to receive.

To what extent is a teacher to be a model to his students? How much should students fashion themselves after him?
Everyone is not the same, and a soul is the result of its experiences. One sheds imitation after a while and, for lack of a better expression, one comes into one's own style.

As our goal is immortality, we may well wonder why we are not given more suffering. All men number four, five, six and seven require friction to keep their work practical, and to change their level of being. Naturally, the machine resents friction instead of trying to transform it, but trying to avoid suffering in itself causes suffering. An old Sufi counsels: "One meets one's fate on the road one took to avoid it." Many areas of work may appear insignificant yet, because they can be transformed, they are blessings. One cannot make a living transforming imaginary suffering because basically, only real suffering produces real results.

Because the level of being of men number four is not uniform, some will have a greater capacity to avoid identification and transform negative emotions than others. I say this because one has one's own being to look to if one expresses negativity, even if it is not expressed in words. One cannot afford to go at the pace of others because valuation for the work can vary considerably.

False personality often considers friction an interruption to its momentum. This is why it is imperative that one not express negative emotions, but transform them and thereby produce higher centers. There is truly no justification for negative emotions. When false personality prevents us from transforming our suffering into being, we have traded something for nothing.

How can we develop the capacity to separate from our negative emotions?
Transforming negative emotions must become a habit; the more you do it the more you can do it. It is a business and a considerable part of good householder.

One of the best ways for a man number four to remember himself is to immediately separate from disappointment that one has not been remembering oneself. One must develop the habit of immediately transforming it into self-remembering.

Negative 'I's plague one, as this is their purpose; one is not intended to be relieved of them. If one is awake, one does not need them, but if one is asleep, one needs all the assistance one can receive. It is a law that one must transform negativity in order to awaken. Johann Goethe said that one should expect the worst until the end; this means that one should expect assistance, or friction, to awaken until one's role closes.

Negative emotions are almost always concerned with something small, which one can allow oneself to magnify out of scale. Blaise Pascal said, "A mere trifle consoles us because a mere trifle distresses us." When something small consoles us, it reveals how small our negative emotions are.

To evolve one must transform the little negative events that occur each day; one can overcome great suffering only by transforming small sufferings. It is wonderful when one can see friction as an opportunity. It is such a strange lifesaver we have been cast by higher forces—the lifesaver of transforming suffering.

I have tried to make awakening as noble and positive an experience as possible, but I said long ago that the angels carry a wand in one hand and a club in the other. One has to transform insidious friction, and this transformation is exactly what Jesus Christ personified.

Tragedies inevitably come to us all, with or without the school, but with the school we can use them, rather than be used by them. Our heart is incredibly resilient, and can rebound from devastating shocks. The biblical story about Daniel in the lion's den depicts World 6 struggling with the emotional center, struggling to transform negative emotions.

John Milton created his astral body before his blindness, and then used his blindness to deepen his level of being. Milton said about his ordeal, "I argue not against heaven's hand." This is one of our finest examples of the transformation of suffering.

Dante Alighieri wrote, "Make fit for mounting to the stars." Separating from and transforming suffering through self-remembering is indeed the passage to the stars for the immortal soul.

There is nothing more noble, nothing of greater importance than inconspicuously transforming negative emotions or suffering. It is such a silent and great struggle we are involved in. Fortunately, we are in favor with higher powers, who are not impressed with life nor with negative emotions. Basically, one's evolution revolves around not expressing negative emotions because this directly encourages self-remembering.

No surer sign of sleep exists than a negative emotion.

When the machine wants to become negative, tell yourself, "Hold your standard." Then one has to get behind the 'I' and be the words. The work 'I's can only advise us; we have to support them. We owe it to ourselves to transform negative emotions.

Imaginary pressures are responsible for many negative emotions, most of which originate in the instinctive center. Remembering to supply the instinctive center with its needs—in moderation—can allay many expressions of negativity. Jesus said: "Render unto Caesar the things which are Caesar's."

It is difficult to remember which angle of thought to apply to a given line of friction because one is struggling to reduce the difference between one's knowledge and one's being; experience enables one to work more efficiently as time passes. It is a miracle to convert water into wine, that is, knowledge into personal understanding. The main key to our work is transforming negative emotions.

There is nothing more difficult for a man number four than transforming negative into positive emotions. The expression of negativity is mechanical, and deeply programmed into our machines. One must therefore allow for failures since certain negative manifestations are so powerful that initially one can only attempt to separate from them.

Is there a practical way to transform negativity?
Externally considering another can stop negativity, as can engaging one's moving center, or reading.

How does one turn the other cheek?
By accepting whatever is in the present. Buddha used to eat whatever fell into his cup. If suffering falls into our cup, we must transform it. So much of our ability to transform negative emo-

tions depends on our main accumulator. If it is worn down, our thinking is worn down and sometimes we are forced into making efforts in a fatigued machine.

Real men and women consume negative emotions. Self-remembering is the only thing that is not eaten—it must eat negative emotions.

We can transform negativity only when we understand that we gain nothing by expressing it and everything by resisting it—all and everything.

What a waste negative emotions will have been to us at the end of our lives—to have used our time that way. When one identifies with suffering and fails to transform it, one has wasted sorrow. It is a noble emotion to feel sad about a shock, but there is a higher response, and that is to transform it. That is where the machine stops and we begin.

We each need to transform suffering throughout our lives. It's difficult when we have so many friends who pass. We understand more and are more involved. Some shocks show us how much potential we have and aren't using. The only way we can do more is to be present. The present has its own rights, one always has the living to serve. There is no dwelling on one's loss. There are no former students that I dislike because one could not be in that plane and be present. Self-remembering and hatred cannot occupy the same space.

Transforming suffering is a pillar of awakening. Feminine domination, identification and inner considering stand between you and your soul. Remorse can be a noble emotion, yet not nearly so noble as transforming remorse. Obviously one must rise above feminine dominance to transform suffering.

If we successfully prevent our machines from buffering the transformation of negative emotions in one area, they will automatically select a new approach to obstruct transformation.

Everyone suffers here, with or without the system, but we get something for ourselves. We are not better than life, just luckier. If one feels guilty about one's luck, one is under feminine dominance. Mr. Ouspensky said luck was the most important variable, and we have the luck to be chosen by Influence C to evolve. Horace said, "The joys I have enjoyed, despite fate, are mine." But actually, it is because of fate. It is not in spite of denying force that we evolve—it is because of denying force. That understanding embraces the whole concept of the transformation of suffering.

Socrates was offered a plan whereby he could escape his sentence of death; he refused by saying that he would rather be innocent before the gods and a victim of men, than resist the demands of higher powers. He concluded by saying, "Leave me then to fulfill the will of the Gods and to follow whither they lead."

Schools are accelerated evolution, and not relative awakening. One changes quite a bit in three to six months, mainly through not expressing negative emotions.

It is difficult to give Influence C something because they are metaphysical beings. One of the highest gifts we can give them is to try to accept suffering, to try to transform it.

We do receive major shocks in our lives, but they are infrequent. We must, however, remain alert to the small shocks in order to transform them. William Shakespeare said, "Some must watch, while some must sleep," and we are people who must watch lest we sleep. What then do we watch for? Small negative emotions that occupy the space of self-remembering. You are in the business of transforming suffering, large or small, to produce your soul.

The machine has many subjective states, but they are illusions that take our time. That is the worst part of it. A negative emotion isn't as innocent as it looks because we pay for it with our time.

One must thoroughly understand the scale that one's machine gives to petty negative emotions. Negativity isn't worth a thing. The non-expression of negative emotions gives one energy. One must discern for oneself what constitutes a negative emotion. The only antidote to negative emotions is remembering oneself.

The more one transforms suffering the closer one is to the end; Christ proved that. No one suffered so much in such a short time. It was the last week of his role that made Christ especially great, his silence under trial. His statement, "Father, forgive them; for they know not what they do," exemplifies the transformation of suffering.

We are here to transcend our wounds, and death proves the transformation of suffering precious. One reason it is difficult to awaken is because we are surrounded by six billion people who are asleep. It is difficult not to imitate their insubstantial being and their empty pursuits. Be present. Marcus Aurelius Antoninus wrote, "What does it matter if the whole world cries out against you, if you are right?"

Awakening has to be difficult, otherwise we wouldn't be interested. On the surface, friction would appear to make a jungle out of evolution. But if one assimilates a shock correctly by transforming it, it brings harmony to one's soul. We naturally grow stronger through transforming friction.

How Influence C softens us.

Really, one can give Influence C hardly anything; an offering of flowers would be much better than gold. They have everything and are everything. The way to pay them back is to not identify with suffering, and to transform it. Then you don't waste your time or theirs.

Relinquishing negative emotions is a matter of life and death. Not only the quantity, but the quality of transforming suffering matters. Suffering itself is a waste, but transforming it is precious. One truly cannot buy anything lasting but self-remembering, and that at the price of transforming suffering.

It is the transforming of suffering that makes everything possible—one can transform suffering and make one's life divine. Our human heart is so great that there is almost no limit to what it can transform.

SCALE AND
RELATIVITY

Everything but self-remembering is nonsense. As one studies the system, the scale of this single idea becomes paramount. No idea can begin to approach the mass of self-remembering, and nothing compares with it.

We have made a breakthrough with self-remembering; it is the idea we have been searching for throughout our lives. Regardless of what action one takes to develop one's essence, one's efforts must also be accompanied by the colossal idea of remembering oneself.

The idea of remembering oneself is most appealing to those who have been disappointed with everything else. When one meets a school, the hidden meaning of life on earth is revealed.

One of the main forces that thwart self-remembering is a lack of valuation for the state, and insufficient valuation is the result of not having established true scale. It will hardly occur to one's machine to try to remember oneself; thus, one must somehow attempt to introduce self-remembering to each moment of the day. Strengthening one's valuation for self-remembering may be a slow process. As one's ability to remember oneself increases, one's valuation will also grow. Men number four may not be able to remember themselves as much as they wish, and yet the more one realizes one's time is limited, the more energy one will devote to it. Thus verification, like all of the other concepts of the system, revolves around self-remembering.

One may be able to extract only moments of self-remembering from a day. Nevertheless, these fragments of reality are one's real possessions. Marcus Aurelius Antoninus, a Stoic Roman emperor and conscious being, wrote in his *Meditations,* "The present is the only thing of which a man can be deprived." Not only must one encounter the idea of self-remembering, but one must learn how to value it. When one cannot value being present, one is deluding oneself, for self-remembering is an incomparable idea.

When two people argue, they usually consider only two opinions. One may be more true, that is, have more scale but, in a state of relativity, both opinions are true. It is understandable that we do not comprehend scale and relativity. It is also imperative that we learn to understand them. Remember yourself regardless of the scale of your activities.

Five to six billion people on the earth have not discovered self-remembering and, what is worse for them, they don't want to hear about it. Self-remembering reveals nature's mistake. It is an intentional flaw—the way out of human bondage.

There is essentially one issue—self-remembering. Shakespeare wrote, "To be, or not to be, that is the question." Each day is important only in relation to the amount of self-remembering one can extract from it.

One of the beautiful aspects of self-remembering is that it is a reward unto itself. We are the luckiest people in the world, and if you don't know it, you should know it.

How can one learn to value oneself without excessively thinking about oneself?
Ironically, you develop your self by not thinking about yourself, by noticing the remarkable impressions outside of yourself, and by external considering. Relativity is the key to understanding. Although our existence corresponds to the level of a cell in the vast universe, we must work with what we have been given.

It seems that the more one knows, the more one does not know.
Our job is not necessarily to know, but *to be*. It is altogether preferable to be a passive force through remembering oneself than to be an active force in sleep. Understanding how little one truly knows is an honest position and a solid place upon which to build.

It is difficult to understand scale.
It's hard but it's so simple. Consciousness has degrees, and you must find ways to increase your consciousness. One has *to be* for oneself. Unlike most concepts, scale and relativity are not formatory, which explains why it is difficult to understand them. Increase your consciousness and scale and relativity will correspondingly increase. The apostle Paul said about his whole incredible life, "What I have suffered is nothing compared to what I have gained." One must give one's life to ideas, and the question is whether they are the correct ideas.

We are people who have entered the way, which is an incredible achievement. Subjects such as alchemy or essence don't mean much compared to entering the way. The only way one can have everything is to be satisfied with self-remembering. It often takes the shock of death to realize this.

People either forget or do not understand that words are only symbols that point to a silent reality. Symbols cease to be important when one discovers self-remembering, which proceeds outside of these ideas. They do not have to come true for us to remember ourselves. We need to talk about theories in order to be prepared. The seconds we gather in self-remembering are not in vain.

Everything is relative and subjective except one's self. When one is present, one is objective. Try to refuse to indulge in, or be swayed by, anything but self-remembering. Esoteric knowledge, contrary to general knowledge, makes us uncomfortable because it reveals our minuscule scale. The machine does not like to have its idea of scale interrupted but, when one is not remembering oneself, it doesn't matter who, or where, or what, one is.

How may one develop a state of relativity so that one can see more of each moment?
You penetrate the present by not thinking of yourself, by avoiding over self-indulgence. You must find other things interesting besides yourself and often hollow pursuits. Milton wrote: "We strive to keep up a frail and feverish being."

Many negative emotions are the result of our inability to establish scale. We identify with trivial events, and perpetuate illusions of reality. Why are we reluctant to establish scale? Because the greater part of our nature is illusory and doesn't want to be reminded of it. What agony we endure when we find ourselves disarmed by imaginary suffering.

It is painful to observe men because they are capable of great achievements, yet they accomplish little. William Blake said, "He who does not keep right onward is lost." If one does not keep moving toward one's aim to awaken, one is lost. In order to discriminate, one must establish scale, and to do this, one must transform suffering.

The greatest secret on earth—self-remembering and divided attention—is so obvious that it's hard to see it as a secret. If you know the secret, do not "throw pearls before swine."

What there is to gain is so great that I relentlessly return to one word: self-remembering. It is an enormous challenge to speak creatively about one word all one's life, but I understand more than you that your life is at stake and I love you, so we must continue and never give up. There is nothing to turn back to, and everything to go forward to.

All one can truly harvest in this life is self-remembering.

Peter Ouspensky said that what the system has that life does not have is scale and relativity. One must give self-remembering the right scale and value it above everything else. We may never excel at anything more than self-remembering. It would be incorrect crystallization to take something as more important than self-remembering.

A useful question to ask oneself is, "Are you remembering yourself now?" If one laments about losing a family relationship, one is reacting as any mechanical man would react. The school has been cast into the twentieth century. We are an enigma to our families because we do not wish a merely biological existence, but a conscious existence.

Jesus said when he was twelve that he must be about his father's business. This does not refer to his age, but to World 12 within him. That is, when World 12 was functioning in him, higher emotional center, he was doing conscious work in the Ray of Creation. One is not of value unless one is remembering oneself. And when we are remembering ourselves, we are of exceptional value to higher forces.

One cannot discount fate when considering the progress of one's evolution. People who enter the way have fate, which means that they can perform no more and no less in this lifetime than their roles dictate.

How can I gain more valuation for self-remembering?
Realizing that one's time is limited and being repelled by one's sleep are two catalysts for increasing valuation for self-remembering. Discovering self-remembering is a mi-fa experience; to value it at any price is a si-do experience.

The subject of conversation is not as important as the need to self-remember. Once, when we were speaking about how to remember a thought while continuing to listen, I suggested that one remember two or three words and then continue listening. If you forget what you wish to say, don't worry. No one has passed through this life without having spoken too much.

It is difficult to remove oneself from nature, yet man has within him that which can surpass the stars. We admire the ancient Greeks because they surpassed nature with a classical ideal. Our contemporary science estimates that there are two hundred and ten billion galaxies in the universe. And yet as small and insignificant as we are, we contain enough to surpass the stars. Omar Khayyam wrote, "That inverted bowl we call the sky, whereunder crawling cooped we live and die, lift not your hands to it for help, for it as impotently rolls as you or I." The stars are a mechanical creation on the order of World 12. We are given essence at birth, that is, World 24. True personality, World 48, is a product of school work, and false personality, World 96, is a result of ordinary influences encountered in life.

God has arranged that the microcosmos man can equal or surpass planets, stars and galaxies in the little amount of time that he has been given. The galaxy is divine machinery, but it is not real. The microcosmos of man is greater when he remembers himself.

One can become lost in innumerable ways, but people get what they want—it is a question of desire. Men number four say, "Why can't I?", which is where understanding stops. They are satisfied with their pace, and the pace of others. Try not to be stopped here.

Keep plunging into the unknown, knowing it is the only direction home. Everything else has to fail because only self-remembering is real and all else mechanical. We must not allow it to become simply a word.

Use difficult subjects as opportunities for remembering yourself. After many years of teaching, I have tired of the novelty of the system except for self-remembering. It is important not to lose the greatness of self-remembering amidst so many other ideas. Only presence is ours—there is never a time to lay it aside. Don't wait until death to verify this.

Self-remembering is a school idea; it is not a concept for the tragic masses out of which we came.

Does one ultimately receive what one wishes?
One receives more than one wishes if one wishes to be present and create an immortal astral body.

Everything on earth is consumed except self-remembering. It seems impossible that this will occur, and yet there is a date for each of our deaths, just as there was a date for our meeting. Everything disappears except self-remembering. The body, Influence A—everything but our moments of consciousness are ruthlessly torn away from us.

One of the greatest equalizing forces in the Ray of Creation is self-remembering, because it does not depend upon anything but oneself. It is the only thing real and the only thing possible. Self-remembering is, in all respects, a godsend. Mr. Ouspensky said, "You do not know the scale of what we are after."

Influence C, our soul and friendship are our three most important possessions. We have the good fortune to be together all our lives. Every day is a blessing, and there is much work to do, wherever one is, accompanied by self-remembering.

There is no possibility of conveying what one gains by self-remembering, and what one loses by not remembering oneself. It will always remain our highest alternative, the summit of scale.

TIME

Time erases all physical phenomena. Even so, one's self remembered is so powerful that it erodes time, which ceases to exist with self-remembering.

We already know that we have created moments in our lives that are out of time, for if each person reviews his life, he will find remembered moments that time cannot erase. Self-remembering is so powerful that it alone can conquer time.

One will become old waiting if one waits for ideal circumstances in which to work.

Jesus said that every hair is counted and nothing is lost. Every second one remembers oneself counts as a hair toward one's astral body. The seconds or moments one can take out of one's day are never lost. Time does not actually exist for our astral body; it is metaphysical.

Every day we are a little less in debt to time, but other people are, every day, more in debt to time. Self-remembering creates a timeless state, an astral body. One *becomes* the fourth dimension, and one is outside of time.

The less time one has, the more strongly one feels the urge to remember oneself because one understands more deeply how little time one has left to awaken.

The older one becomes the more one favors slow growth, for it contains within itself the germ of perfection. All that is great is won slowly.

You will understand Influence C to the greatest extent in the twilight of your life, and will have a greater ability to penetrate the eternal Now.

Esoterically, the cross symbolizes man through time. Man is represented vertically, while time is represented horizontally. Man escapes time through transforming suffering, which is why Jesus Christ was crucified on the cross. Our temporal machines will perish soon. Our moments of self-remembering, however, have already proven themselves out of time. They are of the fourth dimension. To understand the fourth dimension one must be in the fourth dimension. This is one of the great secrets of existence. You will understand it without words as you will have become the words.

We have only a limited number of breaths to take in this lifetime, and we must use them well. Students are generally not late to appointments because they understand that to be out of time they must be on time. It is that simple.

There is no area exempt from self-remembering except the refreshing of accumulators in the first state. One has twenty-four hours each day, six to eight of which we spend in first state refreshing accumulators. This gives one sixteen to eighteen hours in which to try to be present, to experience simple, common moments through divided attention.

Whenever one transforms negativity one surpasses time by entering the timeless realm of higher centers, which are immortal. When one is negative, time has been lost to false personality. If one fails to transform friction, one's time, as well as Influence C's, is consumed uselessly.

I do know that time does not exist for higher centers—the word 'immortality' means just that. The universe is below us, above us, behind us and before us. It is an infinite, omni-directional void. We are creating souls; this is not a poetic fantasy. Influence C has chosen us to evolve, not just to perpetuate humanity by leading a biological existence.

When one is traveling for ten days it can seem like months, because higher centers are functioning, and time seems elongated. We live such a short time and yet, in this brief period, we can create an immortal astral body. It is a mystery of the Absolute.

How brief is our passage through life. We are in a race—not with our fellow men—but with time. It is appalling to witness how man wastes his time. If you have little respect for your own time, you will have little respect for another's. Learn to use your time well, for man's natural inclination is to waste time, chiefly through idle conversation. Mechanical parts of centers wile our time away.

As one's time wanes, it becomes more imperative to *be* the words. It was always urgent; it simply becomes more apparent. The amount of time spent within a school is no guarantee of entering the way. After years, some slowly trudge to a severe interval, while another may pass through the same interval after being in the school for only a few months.

Time, and our unique microcosmos, present us with an opportunity to use them well. Try to develop attitudes whereby you bring a lifetime of care to each waking moment. If you are not awake, you do not have one second to waste, for our years, months and days reduce themselves to few, and our time is not unlimited.

How can one produce enough internal pressure to maintain one's work at a maximum level?
Use inconspicuous voluntary suffering more and ask Influence C for help. The latter, especially, requires courage as friction will be

given for one to transform into an astral body. If the shocks are cruel, remember they love you.

No one ever dies in a state of perfect health. I had to be reckless to break through time—to take chances. Longevity is not the answer, although I hope you will all have long lives to contribute to the school. Still, that is not the answer. While life is indifferently consumed and recycled by eternity, our moments of self-remembering are forever ours. It isn't necessarily how much time we have left that is important, but how we use what remains. Eventually, when one has collected enough moments of self-remembering, one's astral body will fuse.

I have spoken about one word, self-remembering, for more than twenty years. William Shakespeare wrote, "For as the sun is daily new and old, so is my love still telling what is told." It is life or death for you, so I speak relentlessly about this dear old subject.

The year seems like a page turning, and although it has been a long year, the brevity of life is alarming. Must man wait until he is near death in order to understand that all he witnesses lies, and that he has been beguiled most of all by himself? When a little infant is born, his time is almost gone. Even if one lives to be one hundred, it is nothing when set against the vastness of eternity.

It is wonderful that there is something that can defeat time and death. Everything disappears except one's self in the end. Even one's body disappears. That is why one's moments of self-remembering are so precious. Time does not exist and death does not exist when you exist.

If one lives to be 76, one's life is 912 months. It is instructive to view one's life in terms of months rather than years, and to live to be 76 is an achievement. One's entire life emerges as a brief moment. Time, which once marched, suddenly roars by. Everyone is in a race with time, whether they understand it or not.

We are working with great uncompromising laws that only bend with self-remembering and the transformation of suffering.

DEATH

Death is something very few people talk about, or prepare for. Self-remembering alone can confront death, because it uses the same tactics as death, but before the body's demise. Death is one way to see one's nothingness, although there are other ways to understand this before death occurs. In the Fourth Way, one is slowly reduced to a lofty understanding. Rainer Rilke wrote, "It is strange to lay one's own name aside, like a broken toy. It is strange not to continue wishing. Strange to see all relations flutter loosely into space. And it is tiresome not to exist and be full of retrieving, so that one must experience traces of eternity by degrees."

Self-remembering is the only flaw in organic life on earth. It is nature's only mistake, for through self-remembering man can surpass nature by escaping death, which is something nature herself cannot do.

We all know tonight may be our last night. Every day I think of death, not in a morbid way, but of its inevitability, and of preparing for it with self-remembering. One must have a brush with death, or death itself, to experience the emptiness of life. It takes one or the other for us to realize that all we have is self-remembering. After my automobile accident, I realized that I could have died without knowing it, and I understood that most people do die that way. Yet once a student has entered the way of a conscious teaching, even death cannot remove him from the

work. One must make unremitting efforts to return to self-remembering throughout one's life, for unless one attempts to remember
oneself, one is suffering regardless of whether one is happy or sad.
I cleaned my fireplace today and marvelled at all the ashes. That
is our fate very soon, for all of us.

Before our death we must hasten to gather all the consciousness
we can because that is ours, that is what we take with us when the
body expires.

We are in an incredibly dangerous situation and it is important
that we remember ourselves. Everyone in life walks naïvely around
like they are already in heaven or going to heaven. We must use
this vessel that we have to create astral bodies. Our moments of
self-remembering are never lost. The deepest part of our nature
understands that we are preparing for death—it knows and understands ideas that we act as though we don't understand. A
foretaste of death emerges as the years pass. One's time is limited
and diminishing, and the urgency of remembering oneself becomes apparent. In the end, there shall you find the beginning.

Death corners one, and all one has is self-remembering—it is
enough. Death deprives one of everything except one's accumulated moments of self-remembering. People who enter the way
will escape death through their ninth life.

A student "dropped dead" yesterday; he was about fifty, a good
student, lived in a teaching house, and now higher forces have
effected the transmigration of the soul; they took the soul and left
the body crumpled on the floor. This transmigration has taken
place in this century, amidst these sleeping people. The death of
a student reminds us what to work for.

Death is never very far away, and we will all have tombstones over
us soon enough. We only have today, and we may not even have

the rest of that; yet, we can have eternity whenever we are present. Death is an illusion if one crystallizes correctly.

Mr. Ouspensky said that one of the functions of a true psychology is the study of one's limitations. We need to accept our inability to penetrate the idea of recurrence. To verify this concept one may need to study in a school on a higher level than ours, with an astral body only. Although many great men have spoken about recurrence and said that they were certain of the accuracy of this idea, one can study the system apart from it. One can work practically on avoiding recurrence by trying to be present now.

I love my parents, yet I am under no illusions about their fate. Our parents have to die and suffer the fate of all human beings unless they, like us, are trying to be twice born.

I feel the pulse of the end of my role, but, of course, it is the end of the physical body only. Each of us is going to come to the point of death, but our youth conceals that fact. When one is between the ages of 35 and 40, one starts to look into a sunset, whereas before, one was looking at a sunrise. Those are words, and it is a real experience. Walt Whitman said, "An unknown sphere more real than I dream'd, more direct, darts awakening rays about me." Man is the only creature that can understand the magnitude of oblivion.

Once, all the furniture in my room was removed except my bed and a chair, and when I stepped into the room, I realized that death was like that: all one can take with one is one's self. My house was bare. I cannot recall having another experience like this that reduces one to the simplicity of life. Death is a natural transition that we somehow meet positively.

Credentials are deceiving, and death is not impressed by them. Death is an experience, and yet, it is also an illusion. It is like birth: each must go through it.

Solon said, "Call no man happy until he dies." Look at your time that way; don't judge any month until you see how it ends.

Mr.Ouspensky said, "All partings carry the germ of death." That is why we are quite sensitive when we say good-bye to one another, as one never knows when death will occur. Certainly we all will verify this one at a time. Michel de Montaigne said we are all novices when it comes to death. It is impossible to stop the death of the body.

Ordinary people are shocked at death, at the reality that they will die. It is the same for us. Trials force one back upon oneself, to essence, true personality and higher centers. When suffering occurs to one it is a shock—that suffering would be the suffering that it is. Most people buffer it much of their lives with yelling and unnecessary talk. Men do not think they will perish, though they soon will perish. Isn't it amazing how death always disarms us? We're always surprised by it, always shocked, but death is never very far away.

I am just a teacher, not your self. I shall forgive you your faults, and you mine. Death will not, for nothing is more unforgiving than death. Few words can be appropriate to one struggling with death, for an encounter with death reveals how little we know about the fate of our impoverished ruling faculty. Indulgence in self-pity may be foremost yet, in spite of the mammoth pressure to experience this emotion, the alternative accessible to one is to keep penetrating the present until one's life has run its course. The present is all that is truly one's own, and when death challenges us, this becomes obvious.

How do you know that self-remembering has anything to do with death?
Of course, I speak from my own verification—you will have to verify this for yourself, and the reality that invisible beings, Influence C, are helping us to escape. Try to remember to think in terms of "how" instead of "why." Death takes everything from us

but our moments of presence. We cannot verify this now, but according to the system, at death an energy field flies to the moon, or World 96, and Mr. Gurdjieff said that infinitely long planetary cycles must elapse before the opportunity of escape presents itself again.

Eventually, one becomes the oldest one in the room. One can feel the final farewell, when one lays aside this mortal body.

At death, one is reduced to the utter simplicity of one's being. The point of death will come for each of us, and man number four will put his soul in the hands of Influence C (into thy hands I commend my spirit) and hope that they will place him in limbo to await a conscious role. Everything points to this. Socrates said that when one dies, if one is not crystallized, one's soul is placed in limbo, a divine state of rest. Nightmares and dreams will not interrupt the state of limbo. Purgatory is a state of punishment. Most of us have verified that Influence C exists, which strongly suggests that purgatory exists. Limbo would be for ascending souls; a cradle for the soul, a sleep without dreams.

By the grace of Influence C, I have made it through to the other side and will take my students with me.

One does have the immeasurable good fortune of establishing a connection with the miraculous, which is a great comfort, insofar as one can be consoled in such a monumental struggle. Death's struggle reveals how great our illusion of life is. One may not conquer death in this life, yet one may master it in another. Death is not a concern of ours if we crystallize correctly. Between now and then we will have escaped the grave. We are people who have defeated time and death.

Benjamin Franklin's last words were, "A dying man does nothing easily." With self-remembering, one must do everything intentionally, even brushing one's hair.

Death proves that the waste of time is the greatest of crimes.

Most students have little understanding that their machines are destined to expire. They think that life can proceed indefinitely. Even humanity is not immortal and is periodically expunged by higher forces. One of the most important things that one can learn is that the answer is not words, but a state. A person becomes very quiet just before death, because time has run out for false personality.

We are so fortunate that we have everything we need. We have our aim to awaken, we have Influence C lifting us, and we have our sacred school. School on earth is a rare privilege and honor. Those who have left the school are far worse off than those who will never have the privilege of meeting it. If one loses the school, one loses the way because there is nothing left but the first line of work. One needs the second and third lines of work and Influence C to evolve. The safeguard for not losing the school is the knowledge that one needs the school. We are not here to gather comfort from large numbers of people being in the school. Each person is here for himself, heading irrevocably toward the points of birth and death: the birth of the astral body and the death of the physical body. Nothing escapes but consciousness. What else could?

On the Brink of Death

Now hath my life across a stormy sea
Like a frail bark reached that wide port where all
Are bidden, ere the final reckoning fall
Of good and evil for eternity.

Now know I well how that fond fantasy
Which made my soul the worshipper and thrall
Of earthly art, is vain; how criminal
Is that which all men seek unwillingly.

Those amorous thoughts which were so lightly dress'd,
What are they when the double death is nigh?
The one I know for sure, the other dread.
Painting nor sculpture now can lull to rest
My soul that turns to His great love on high,
Whose arms to clasp us on the cross were spread.

Michelangelo Buonarroti

The third state of consciousness is imperishable, and fortunate is
the man who early discovers that being present is his sole possession. This becomes more obvious when one's time begins to wane.
Death's trial is not the time to learn certain profound lessons, such
as understanding that one's time is limited. One must understand
devastating laws as quickly as possible in order to take measures
to escape them.

We are all heading for the point of death, and are doing something
about it now. In attempting to escape death, we are involved in a
far greater war. It was difficult for Johann Goethe to have lived so
long. Yet he said, "The last and greatest art is to limit and isolate
oneself." Death is a one-to-one experience whereby two forces,
death and one's self, struggle for control. One outwits death by
remembering oneself.

Most aged people creep toward death helpless and complaining.
We, too, will die, but not like them. We must do our best not to
complain and to transform the ultimate experience, the final act.

Dinner is often the summation of the day. And one day it will be
the summation of a life; that is, we will end our roles on one
particular day. We sit here lively and attentive, but it is all tentative
except for self-remembering.

People who pursue Influence A die a shallow death without
acquiring something for themselves. There is no deceiving death.

It will not accept credentials or medicines. The one thing that obstructs death is self-remembering. There will come for each of us a day when one will freeze in one's tracks, when one sees death on one's own face.

It will be because of experiences we share that students will not taste death. That is, through the course of nine lives will come success. We work all our lives to remember ourselves. When death arrives, we do not lose; we keep the best of what we have garnered; it passes to another vessel. Nature, with its incredible cycle of life and death, teaches one to mature. Death extracts an enormously heavy toll both from those who perish, and those who remain. We, who remember, will the remembered be. The ancient Greeks spoke of the cemetery in our heart, which we must each carry.

There are five to six billion people on the earth now and all will fall prey to time. We are people who have been given the privilege of transcending time. I hope to give my finest knowledge to you when my task is complete. I am almost certain that higher forces will allow contact, and at that time I hope to pass information to you regarding your next life, and to advise you that death is in all respects an illusion for ascending souls. This remains a theory for us tonight; nevertheless, it may be a fact for higher school.

One takes one's love for the gods, God and one's soul from this plane of existence. All we have to do is divide attention to avoid death. Self-remembering is its own reward, and each of our deaths will verify these words. Death is the end of life and eternal life the end of death.

Consciousness

One may understand something clearly today and not comprehend it tomorrow, because consciousness has degrees. Although one may be dissatisfied with the result of one's efforts for a series of days, one must remember to view the work from the point of view of years, and even lifetimes. The school is successful and it produces consciousness in its participants.

The more fully one understands that one is asleep, the more one will be repelled by it and will desire to awaken. One of the most helpful catalysts for awakening is the realization of how repugnant sleep is.

It is interesting to consider where one goes when one is not remembering oneself. One quietly disappears, robbed by the thief of imagination. There is such a fine shade between the first and second states of consciousness, and the same delicate line exists between the second and third states. This is why simple shocks will often produce higher states in us. We are fortunate our machines are balanced so delicately that we can readily enter immortal realms.

Nature does not encourage one's aim to awaken, and has arranged a variety of alluring, yet vacuous deviations. Awakening is a simple matter. Divided attention is simultaneously being aware of oneself and what one is looking at. It is the state that we seek day after day. The path to being is circuitous, not direct. Michel de Montaigne said we are like a drunken man staggering toward his goal.

There are many lamps to guide one on one's painful path, yet there are few who wish a light to penetrate their darkness. We are people who have committed themselves to awakening. That is why we are here this evening, rather than elsewhere.

One cannot have conscience without consciousness. In the full meaning of the idea, a machine cannot have a conscience. Regardless, one must work with what one has. It is necessary to be in a state of relativity to understand the ideas of the system.

One has to make efforts, and trying to be present takes one closer to the third state of consciousness. Sometimes efforts to be present push one into the present. Influence C carries a wand in one hand and a club in the other, and we feel both throughout our gestation. They have to club a man number four because subtle shocks don't work. It's through both the mystical moments and the Herculean moments that we verify—and more importantly, become—the work.

The third state is our true identity. Higher centers are always quite close.

What are some characteristics of the third state?
One characteristic is simplicity. The third state of consciousness is not cold or aloof, although it is a wordless realm. Certain vacuous states try to possess one's being, but they are not one's self. The instinctive brain is opposed to self-remembering and will undermine one's work by trying to find flaws in the rarest gem on earth, one's precious self. Higher centers are represented in the Bible as children in order to symbolize their innocent state.

The third state is uncomfortable, yet satisfying. When the third state makes its appearance, accept it. There is nothing finer that you can accept than your self.

The third state is none of the 'I's, it is one's soul. The best work 'I's are not it—consciousness is not functions. One has to find ways to grip and perpetuate the present. Use the looking and listening exercises, and above all, transform suffering. One cannot be negative and *be*.

The work 'I's that instruct one to remember oneself are still not one's self, remembering. The precious work 'I', "Be present," is not the state of presence, although it is definitely closer to one's self than many formatory statements such as, "Hello, how are you?" One can be closer to the shores of the third state of consciousness or further away, and work 'I's are quite near the shores of the third state. Mechanical 'I's are near the first state, and there is little of value behind them.

The first time I entered St. Peter's Cathedral, my king of hearts began to experience an ecstatic, religious emotion, the closest mechanical emotion to the experience of one's self. Immediately I had to choose self-remembering over self-indulgence. As a result, I experienced the third state.

We are always trying to focus on self-remembering, trying to break through the veil of imagination. One positive aspect of large shocks is that they lift the veil of imagination, the third state appears and won't go away. Angels are technicians who can create brilliant shocks. One either uses the shocks or gets used by them. A strong shock will not disappear—it leaves the third state of consciousness resounding in one.

Humiliation produces the third state—one's humble soul. One must experience humiliation often throughout one's life to create one's astral body.

Without self-remembering, without the third state, confusion reigns. Remember to use common sense.

The attempts to produce an objective state prove difficult because the second state of consciousness seems real to one when compared to the relatively lifeless first state. Such a deception can prevent one from experiencing consciousness.

Awakening is much more than you can imagine because it is not imagination, it is reality. It's important to take Influence C on their terms. Whatever they give you, try to bear it evenly. If you want to awaken, nothing will stand in your way; if you don't want to awaken, you will stand in your own way.

It is useful for us to live as long as we can to serve Influence C. It is the nature of an ark to endure when humanity self-destructs.

Could you speak about conscious hope?
Dante said that on the gates of Hell was written "Abandon all hope, ye who enter here." Someday the entrance of Apollo shall read, "Nourish all hope, ye who enter here." Awakening transports one beyond hope, and one learns to accept *what is* as one verifies one's inability to alter external circumstances. Also, the more conscious one is, the less one would wish to modify this impoverished dimension of the Ray of Creation called Earth. The last item remaining in Pandora's box was hope. This suggests that in developing, many unpleasant observations are recorded during one's ascent from the allurement of Influence A to the pain of Influence B. At this stage, all one has is hope, since awakening is impossible without the outside assistance of Influence C and remember, we have sought and found the miraculous.

If one is awake, one can love; if one is asleep one cannot love.

How can we strengthen that small part in us that is interested in awakening?
Apply positive third forces to your life, balance your three lines of work, or spend more time with students.

We receive shocks because we are asleep; they have no other meaning. We are always in trouble, it's simply a question of becoming aware of it. Self-remembering must be more persistent than sleep.

Sleep is the foe of the gods, and alas, thou art the sleeper.

How can we increase our desire to awaken?
By understanding that awakening is a realizable idea. Remember, sleep makes everything worse and self-remembering makes everything better.

Our school is basically centered on *how* to awaken and not *why* to awaken, because it is self-evident—one is asleep.

One must remember that consciousness is not mind activity.

One must be sincere with oneself and remember that one's soul is in a machine. One must remember it throughout one's life. As one attempts to self-remember, one accumulates certain substances that one uses toward further awakening. Awakening is not for a machine, but for the soul imprisoned in the machine. It is an old idea, and in each century a group of people gather together to share esoteric knowledge and to take appropriate measures to escape.

Ours is the good fortune to be creating souls together and separately. Our first birth is mechanical; our second, conscious. We are twice-born through divided attention. Men number one, two and three lead a biological existence as one generation endlessly replaces another. We have disturbed the peace of our families by discovering self-remembering, yet our role is a gift to our family heritage, although we cannot expect them to appreciate it.

The intensity and duration of one's work will determine the level of one's development. When one attempts to self-remember, and an hour later awakens to discover that mechanical 'I's have been in control, one has an observing 'I'. If a civil war is occurring internally, however, one possesses a steward. A fully developed steward would require a fully developed master. Control would then be issuing from one's self through one's steward. Awakening takes much more patience than one would imagine. We have no choice—do prisoners have a choice?

Awakening consumes naïve enthusiasm because one must be consistent. One may have an emotional realization, but in order to understand an idea permanently, one must be conscious. Sometimes the emotional center is the only center that understands, yet we need all four centers for true understanding, which will come later. To awaken one must transcend the spectrum of the emotional center, as one cannot trust any emotional aim that is not related to awakening.

Although it is a rare exception to form a steward, such a level of development is available to a man number four. A steward does not merely photograph false personality, it controls it with relative success. One would not wish a steward permanently controlling one's machine, however, because one would have no need of one's self, or master. A steward is a mechanism that is designed into one's machine with limitations. It is not intended to control difficult situations because a certain intensity is needed to produce higher centers; one's self, not one's steward, is intended to become conscious.

The raven is a creature designed to serve as a mirror for man, because it gathers trinkets and considers them precious. Similarly, false personality pursues insubstantial aims, and values them above the effort to remember oneself. As John Milton wrote, "Men attribute over much to things less excellent, as thou thyself perceivest. For what admir'st thou, what transports thee so?"

The non-expression of negative emotions is the major key to awakening. A difficult negative emotion to surmount is the identification with one's inability to remember oneself, yet a properly developed steward will prevent such subtle negativity from hindering one's further efforts to awaken.

Consciousness is not mechanical, and thus it must be earned. By making the payment of transforming suffering to awaken, one understands the need for payment. What a pitiful idea it is to wish something for nothing. We are all naïve to the requirements of awakening—it comes down to being crucified innumerable times.

Although youth likes to make efforts to awaken through the body, higher centers awaken through transforming emotional suffering. Still, we try to make awakening as positive as possible. Take nothing seriously but your aim to awaken; don't count on anything but the present.

One can be in the first state of consciousness while one is in the second state. One may observe people in this condition—they are simply absent, they are not moving and their heads are fixed. Mr. Ouspensky concluded the first chapter of his book, *The Psychology of Man's Possible Evolution,* with the statement that there can be consciousness without functions. There can also be functions without consciousness—a man number one, man number two or man number three, as well as each of us when we are asleep. Our machines function without consciousness if we are not remembering ourselves. The third state and the second state can also coexist. Higher centers can and do appear in one while the machine is still regulating itself. For instance, one can simply be placing a log in the fireplace and create the third state.

I am grateful for the many diagrams in the work books, but I don't pursue them because consciousness is not functions, and one would need to pursue them with the intellectual center, which is a function. Of course, the mind has its place. Yet one can do well with or without these diagrams; it primarily depends upon the expression of one's essence. Mr. Ouspensky and Mr. Collin did quite well *with* them.

There is a time to try to avoid all 'I's, even work 'I's. The instinctive center can manipulate work 'I's, causing one to analyze rather than to experience the present. The looking and listening exercises are the best ways to assist one's awakening.

How can we learn to relax?
We are not necessarily here to relax. Christ said, "The son of man [World 6, higher mental] hath not where to lay his head." Remember not to take the wrong things seriously, and this will enable you to experience right work of centers.

Awakening must become an art form, because there is an art to each moment. It is often a simple art form, such as appreciating a tree, a concert or the common moments of friendship. We have to work to be present during our meetings. Those 'I's we generate that say "Awaken" move us closer to the third state of consciousness. When we have a day in which we have experienced an incredible portion of the third state we begin to see what is possible to extract from our existence. The third state is not natural to man—it is metaphysical.

Surges of esoteric knowledge draw us closer to consciousness, yet one cannot encompass all wisdom here, far from it. Consciousness is not functions, nor is it the knowledge we press on our centers. The school surpasses our dreams because it delivers us to reality. The present is the only experience one encounters in one's life that cannot be overrated.

Schools are not designed for relative awakening, they are designed for complete awakening. Influence B *is* relative awakening and relies upon the symbols of identity rather than upon identity itself. Complete awakening is reserved for a man number seven. In a man number six the eternal flame is ignited, but wanes. It requires years to keep it fully flowing. Alexander von Humboldt, Goethe's friend, said, "Nature holds up to God nothing so high as the finished man."

Higher forces will not give the gift of awakening to those who consistently place themselves first. One must be capable of the second and third lines of work, in addition to the first line of work. Esoterically, "the last shall be first" means that those who can serve will experience oneness; those who selfishly place themselves first will be the last in the Ray of Creation and will dwell upon the moon. There are no advantages to any alchemy, center of gravity, sex, weight, age, race or body type. We are speaking about machinery that is capable of producing self-remembering. But what prevents you from thinking so? It is interesting that some people awaken because they imagine it can be done, whereas others do not because they imagine it cannot.

There would be no need for me to remain here if people were not attempting to awaken. An older student and I were speaking before dinner. She remarked that she had been in the school thirteen years and she was not conscious. I replied that because she knows that, she is ahead of all of humanity. You see, we are very close to the exit to eternal life, and we are preparing to leave. I have the greatest respect for my students because they work so much in the dark. I would not begin to teach if I did not know that there was light at the end of the tunnel.

You must make a total commitment to awakening. It's difficult with that commitment, and impossible without it. Think of all the incredible plays that have taken place throughout humanity's history, and then think of your own divine play of becoming conscious. Self-remembering—consciousness—is the hidden meaning of the Ray of Creation, and the reason for our existence. Humanity, the other planets, the sun and the galaxies all serve as a backdrop for self-remembering and creating astral bodies. Conscious beings must be produced in order for the Ray of Creation to grow; the Absolute needs assistance.

When higher centers are functioning, one is awake. Later one's state will descend, and in sleep one cannot remember some elements of the incident, because the lower is attempting to recall what the higher experienced. We must remember that the human machine is exceptionally complicated, and little is known of its operations. Mr. Ouspensky perceived this when he stated that anatomy is an incomplete science. For example, physicians do not know there is an intellectual center, an emotional center, an instinctive center and a moving center. Additionally, each of these four minds is subdivided into three parts: the intellectual, the emotional and the mechanical divisions, represented in the deck of cards by the king, queen and jack, respectively. The jack is further differentiated into the moving and instinctive parts, which initially should be considered as one brain, but later observed as two brains. When one attempts to self-remember, the king of hearts—the intellectual part of the emotional center— functions, and thus is the most noble instrument of the machine except one's self. One's soul, which is located between one's holy temples in the pineal gland, is not of one's machine because it is an astral, rather than a physical, body.

One has groups of 'I's that definitely have verified Influence C, and one has groups of 'I's that don't even know what day it is.

Our degree of consciousness is higher than normal now. We can speak about certain ideas now that we cannot speak of later because the machine will descend to a lesser degree of consciousness. It may even try to become negative. Right now we are pushing

Worlds 12 and 6, but if we are struggling with negative emotions, it means World 96 is pressing on us.

Throughout the day our consciousness varies, and we can even experience a great flux within one minute. Our machines can be buffering one moment and dividing attention the next.

The same great ideas will be repeated throughout the history of the school. What idea can compare with self-remembering? Additionally, some people possess a greater ability to collect knowledge than others. If one wishes to gather more knowledge, one must change one's level of being. But it is not so much that more knowledge is needed; it is that one needs to assimilate what has been given. We cannot say too much that is new because the struggle remains the same in any century: one must labor to create a soul.

I accept quiet pauses during a dinner, although they can be uncomfortable, to remind us that consciousness is not functions. We cannot talk our way out. Learning to bear the discomfort produced by silence is a necessary step in one's development.

Something quite deep within us wishes consciousness to be functions, to be mind activity, but it is not. Awakening is mathematical. The intellectual part of the emotional center functions with hydrogen 12; to awaken, hydrogen 12 must circulate within one's machine as it is conscious material and provides the substance for consciousness, memory and will. It is an electronic hydrogen and is difficult to bear.

Does crystallization begin through self-remembering?
Crystallization begins with the process of self-remembering, which alters one's inner chemistry. Without this system, man generally dwells in mechanical parts of centers. Self-remembering activates emotional and intellectual parts of centers, and establishes reins between the centers and the pineal gland. If one is fated

to crystallize in this life it occurs, in my experience, within ten years. One should just record that. Being a teacher is an inexact science.

The intellectual center cannot become conscious because consciousness is not a function. Our four lower centers try to figure this out; they are like the step-sisters in "Cinderella." Consciousness has degrees, and one of the degrees is that it is permanent. If one is truly self-remembering, one is conscious, although the clarity of one's presence does vary.

If the system did not bend itself to the subjectivity of man, all of the conscious beings it produced would be the same, which would defeat one of the purposes of consciousness. The system itself does not exist. The consciousness produced in its participants is its real achievement. What a mystery existence is! We have many answers but it is still a mystery because consciousness is not functions. Consciousness is a state, not an opinion.

We describe and define, yet consciousness remains consciousness. A swan knows a swan when it beholds one.

HIGHER CENTERS

The presence of higher centers is a reward sufficient unto itself, as they exist in the eternal Now.

The system can only be understood—and withstood—from higher centers.

Self-remembering makes one a different order of creation. Trying to establish a connection with one's own higher centers is much more difficult than anything one has previously attempted because the soul is conscious and not mechanical; thus the process of awakening bears the title of the "Master Game."

One of the secrets of awakening is that higher centers cannot be evoked if one is thinking about oneself too much. Higher centers, when they are produced within us, unselfishly serve. We cannot develop immortal states that are selfish, because they would be a curse to the universe rather than a blessing. For higher centers to come into being we must have the strength of external consideration. Generally, when we attempt to externally consider one another, our machines become so eager that, for example, there may be one chair and two people, and neither sits down. We need to be flexible in order to know when to receive and when to give. Leonardo da Vinci said, "I never tire of serving."

Higher centers have a humble beginning. When one first experiences them, which may be for five seconds, a simple presence without words peers from one's machine.

Higher centers cannot appear if you are heedless of others. External consideration is practical and humane. Look for it in the small, as well as the great, and the divine harmony that resounds throughout the universe will echo within you.

I was sorting over my notes this evening, revising and editing and eliminating, and I noticed, when one fourth of the way through the file, that the word 'I' was only used once. It is a law that higher centers can emerge only if one forgets oneself. One's life becomes more interesting to the extent that one doesn't speak about oneself or think about oneself.

Higher centers cannot come into being when one is immersed in imaginary problems. If one can abandon this shallow tendency of one's being, higher centers can be realized. Asking too many questions about one's work prevents one from seeing what this phenomenal world has to offer. In order to awaken, one has to forget about one's machine and its imaginary sense of importance. Then a compassionate state will eventually develop that is accustomed to thinking about others. There was once a Zen student in Japan who approached his master and said that he had many problems. The master politely asked him to place the problems in his hand. The student couldn't, because his problems were not real. Problems exist on a narrow plane of identification.

Are we actually creating souls by trying to remember ourselves?
Precisely. That is the meaning of life on earth; everything else is biological. William Wordsworth wrote "the child is father of the man." With self-remembering, the man is father of his child— higher centers.

Different energies, such as those from the instinctive center and lower parts of the emotional center, will masquerade as one's self. One's true identity is to be found in the moments that one remembers in one's life, for when memory was functioning, one's higher centers were present. The highest ideas cannot be understood by the four lower centers, but are reserved for higher centers.

The third state is so unexpected. It's foreign because it is so real, while so much of our nature is mechanical. Fortunately, we can find ways to introduce emotional shocks that create the energy needed to develop higher centers. Higher centers have their own intelligence, and their own ways of receiving information.

Awakening is a mathematical process, and results are proportionate to one's efforts. Those who enter the way are involved in a long and diligent struggle for their selves. If it requires ten to fifteen years to become an accomplished artist, what then to create one's self? The many 'I's sometimes remind one of ocean waves that just keep beating one. Sometimes the seventh and largest wave breaks, and one is showered with 'I's. The ruling faculty—one's soul—has a great advantage that the many 'I's can never begin to match. The many 'I's are not real, and the ruling faculty is real.

The knowledge we share is powerful because reality is a foreign experience. You understand this when you establish a brief connection with higher centers.

There is no easy way to higher centers. Whether one awakens in the East or the West, one's trials are difficult: Buddha and Socrates both died of poison. Distinguished men are martyred so that humanity will cultivate the principles they upheld.

Do the higher emotional and higher intellectual centers constitute the self?
Yes. One's soul is a unified being, rather than only male or only female, as the machine is. Plato said people are halves that seek

their opposites. Higher emotional center and higher intellectual center are labels for divine states.

The only way to discover one's true identity is by experiencing higher centers. It is such a vivid experience that a sound person won't forget it. False personality will punish one for experiencing higher centers. The witch in "Snow White" represents one's queen of hearts and she tries to eliminate Snow White, or higher centers, because she wants to be the "fairest one of all."

In general, World 6 is present in times of danger and World 12 in emotional situations. With advanced preparation, World 6 can be present in emotional situations and World 12 in difficult ones.

One way to perpetuate higher centers when they emerge is to accept them. When higher centers appear, one's machine will attempt to dispose of them quickly. False personality might even suggest photographing one's instinctive center, which is quite reluctant to be photographed. One's machine is desperate to undermine the birth of higher centers.

It is not easy for men number four and five to accept higher centers when they appear, because their machines try to undermine higher centers through fear, indifference or a variety of deceptions.

Higher centers sustain themselves as the self remembers to be awake. Additionally, efforts to remember oneself accrue and higher centers may crescendo for fifteen minutes before their ability to be present is exhausted. At such times, one must return to one's steward, for it will prevent one from descending too far.

Certain states are legitimate, but also naïve. Higher centers can be quite lucid, clear and sharp, and they can be progressing without one realizing it. Most importantly, they can be present without shocks. Eventually higher centers begin to educate themselves, because we do not wish to produce something immortal that is not intelligent. As higher centers begin to function, they are like naïve little infants, and one is simply grateful for their arrival. Later the same state reads books and listens to music—it starts educating itself. I am not referring to educating essence, but to higher centers in connection with essence. Higher centers are designed to serve humanity. When higher centers appear they begin with the first line of work, that is, they begin for themselves. When people meet a school, they are expected to work almost exclusively on the first line of work, and later, when they can start thinking of others, they work on the second or third line. When higher centers first appear, they exist for themselves, and later they exist to serve others.

We are fortunate that there is a way out, and that we can use higher parts of centers to reach higher centers. Some students thrive upon pressure, while others wilt, yet the pressure must incessantly flow. Pressure, and only pressure, can draw forth one's latent higher centers.

Higher centers are the fourth dimension of our machines and are not mechanical. The fourth dimension can only be penetrated by *being*. That is, one must *be* the fourth dimension to understand the fourth dimension. One of the reasons that time sometimes seems to pass so rapidly is that higher centers are occasionally present, and time doesn't exist for higher centers; that is, higher centers are out of time.

How can we learn to endure higher hydrogens?
Higher hydrogens are synonymous with one's self or higher centers. To sustain higher centers, one must be able to control the lying of the four lower centers. Each of the four lower functions eagerly ascends, preventing higher centers from manifesting. Furthermore, each possesses an identity of its own, which is negligible compared to one's self.

We have an imaginary picture of what we are, which is far different from reality. We can see our level of being by observing the level of identification that reduces us. The struggle to resist small subjects of identification constitutes our real inner life. Mr. Ouspensky observed that the being of men differs, and that most people have not heard of the idea of self-remembering. He also said that the concept of self-remembering is almost completely overlooked by Western psychology. The idea of being present is, however, expressed in Western poetry, a common theme of which is the appreciation of the moment. Still, we can observe that most poets don't really value this idea—they write just as easily about other things as they do about being present. Nevertheless, we can't reject them for their lack of scale, because some elements of their writings are useful and poignant.

Self-remembering outlives galaxies and stars. Hydrogens 6 and 12 are clinical labels for one's embryonic soul. Each time we suffer a shock we produce a trace of this imperishable, divine substance. Apollo ruling the four horses that pull his chariot esoterically refers to World 6 controlling the four lower centers.

Mr. Ouspensky said hydrogen 48 is like a blank sheet of writing paper. Nothing happens when we look at it; it is neutral. Self-remembering is hydrogen 12 or 6, and it is not neutral. Hydrogen 24 is the dearness of essence. This room and the beautiful columns, urns, sconces, friends and music are obviously noble hydrogens. A beautiful view of nature, like our vineyard, is organic life on earth—hydrogen 24. A street in a modern city with neon lights is hydrogen 96—false personality. So the vineyard is true personality for the earth.

In a day, if you self-remember for one second, two seconds, one minute, or to whatever extent, you pierce infinity. Be grateful for those moments rather than being negative for not being present more often. Of it all, these seconds are what is counted, imperishable, forever yours, you!

One must patiently allow for time to align one's being with one's knowledge. Being present functions at the speed of light, and nothing approaches one's own inner light.

What is the relationship between the reliability of a man number four and conscious love?
Being reliable means not deviating from the aim that gives one life—to awaken. Remember that love spelled backwards means evolve.

One would think that such small bodies as comets wouldn't disrupt the solar system, but it is very delicately balanced. Our higher centers are so delicate and light, yet they can control the four lower centers. Higher centers have a great advantage because they are real, whereas the machine is not. Higher centers don't take the manifestations of machines as individuality.

The senses are needed to produce higher centers. Looking at nature or listening to music can evoke higher centers.

The mind is not the soul. Men are not as alive as we think they are, and if we see them from higher centers, much is unreal. With higher centers functioning, it is like being able to see among blind men—it is truly that different.

When higher centers emerge, they do their best not to be seen. It is difficult to avoid becoming a recluse because higher centers wish a quiet life. One needs both to be by oneself, and to be with others. When higher centers awaken they must serve. George Sand said, "Humanity is not interested in a man if that man is not interested in humanity."

Every second that one is present is added to one's immortal soul, and everything begins with being present. Without self-remembering, one is governed by the law of accident. Every day, we resume the relentless struggle to unencumber the present, to clear the fog of imagination. Influence C gives one difficult 'I's to jar one from imagination, but one learns to use negative thoughts by transforming them. The present is all one ever has, and it is forever one's own.

Higher centers mean love, will and consciousness—there cannot be one without the others.

Self-remembering creates higher centers, which know no time. When higher centers function, time ceases to exist. When one discovers that one's time is limited, it passes more quickly. Time will have its way and compress our life into a few seconds. We will have the last word, however, by creating our soul.

Few people are interested in soaring to the lofty realms of their soul, but we must sacrifice everything for our immortal soul, since schools are not designed for relative awakening.

Higher centers observe the world as it is, without thought patterns. Moments in which one experiences higher centers are imperishable. Try to understand the magnitude of this idea—it means one can be immortal, because there is no ending for an ascending soul.

The soul is greater than the objects it views. To *see* the whole, one must *be* the whole, as higher centers must be functioning.

Immortality is within our reach. Books educate us, but only self-remembering makes us immortal.

THE ASTRAL BODY

Mr. Ouspensky reminds us that we are pursuing something large—the creation of an astral body.

We are a young school in touch with higher school. Influence C communicate how to develop an astral body by not expressing negative emotions, balancing centers and not being in imagination, but they also communicate knowledge that is less intellectual. They have given us some prophecies that are facts to them but, until they turn into facts for us, they must be called prophecies.

It is fitting that awakening is a long process, because nothing approaches it in value. Nothing should take more time than the creation of an astral body.

We have discovered the hidden meaning of life on earth: to create an astral body through divided attention. We are fortunate that we know what to do with our lives. One can't prevent others from wasting theirs, and if one tries, one is wasting one's own.

Self-remembering not only saves time, but creates an astral body not subject to time. Rodney Collin said the work has to be viewed from the point of view of lifetimes. Our bodies will be the same in recurring lives, but our higher centers will have played our roles successfully and will ascend to new roles. The old roles will recur, but we will not be playing them again. One ascends Jacob's

Ladder. You know something good is happening if Influence C is working with us because it clearly means heaven exists, and life after death exists.

Man's wish to fly is a mechanical substitute for creating an astral body. One can only truly fly through self-remembering, as one can create an astral body capable of independent movement throughout the universe. William Shakespeare wrote, in his forty-fourth sonnet, "For nimble thought can jump both sea and land, as soon as think the place where he would be."

As we awaken we become grateful for those who have created astral bodies, because conscious beings don't live *through* others, but *for* them. Being present leads to the crystallization of an astral body, the formation of an immortal soul. We were not present to our physical birth, but we are present to the birth of our astral body.

We know that one cannot exist for another, and that each person must pay to create his astral body. Everything we have is borrowed, even our body. It is mathematically impossible to take anything with us at death other than our soul. Sometimes students will be walking along, and I stop them and tell them that by dividing attention we can create an astral body and escape organic life on earth. Remembering ourselves for three seconds or longer will add to our astral body, our souls. It is a fact that we can create an astral body out of this physical body. There are many parallels in nature: a caterpillar producing a butterfly, an acorn an oak tree. The transformation of a caterpillar into a butterfly is the poetry of the gods. Influence C is pressing firmly on us to produce our astral bodies. This is not a fantasy, but reality.

Did you once say that the astral body could levitate?
Yes. It breathes, in its own divine way, apart from the physical body.

The seasons are an illusion that does not exist for astral bodies.

Mr. Ouspensky said that the system discourages faith, but there exists a place for faith as well as for verification. One of our students said: "Faith is the result of our verifications." The last line of "The Dedication to Faust" reads: "What has vanished now comes into being." To me that means that the soul is freed from the body. What has vanished is Goethe's physical body, and what now comes into being is his astral body. From that same poem is the line, "Still does my heart that strange illusion prize?" Without self-remembering one's life is an illusion; with it, one's life is reality.

How does time cease to exist? It seems that it still exists but only changes.
When you are present you break through time and it ceases to exist. When it seems only to change, you haven't completely lifted the veil of imagination. You are creating an astral body through self-remembering, and it is different from the physical body. Eventually, higher forces will fuse your astral body and time will not exist for it. It doesn't matter if one doesn't understand, because self-remembering is always right action.

Our school is a practical school, concerned with *how* to form an astral body, not *why*. It is important to consider theoretical knowledge, but selectively.

Our astral bodies need to receive natural impressions in order to evolve. The essence of the school is becoming more clear—it is developed through discrimination, learning what to seek and what to avoid. Beauty feeds our astral body. Friedrich Schiller said men must be taught that beauty is a necessity. Nature is beautiful but alluring, and man must journey beyond it to the astral world of his self. Few men understand what they are capable of attaining.

The simple truth is that when one divides attention, one is creating an astral body. The present is everything. We can transform our physical body with an astral body.

Christ's astral body rose from the dead: humanity. We have nine lives, the last immortal. Our astral bodies will be taken by angels while our physical bodies will be left to decay. A man number four must rely on the faith that Influence C will take his astral body upon his death and prepare it for his next role.

THE SELF

The soul has many names, among them: one's self, the master, real 'I', higher centers, higher mental and higher emotional centers, God, the Son of Man, the Kingdom of Heaven, the witness, the third eye and the ruling faculty.

One has to be taught to recognize one's soul and then to value it above all else. Throughout one's life, there are endless lessons without words that are designed to reach one's soul and bypass one's intellectual center.

You can take nothing eternal from this plane except your self.

How tumultuous and pathetic our inner life is. The looking exercise is one of the best ways to interrupt this chaos. One can look at the flowers or the grain in the wood of the table. We are all sometimes exhausted by the 'I's. What observes or, better yet, ignores them, is one's self.

Nothing that we can see is real. We confuse the physical form with life, but there is nothing real except self-remembering, although the machine mistakenly thinks it is real.

We have enemies and allies within us; only you stand between you and your soul.

One inwardly searches for something one has forgotten during the day. Then, with alarm, one realizes that one has forgotten oneself.

How can one be more responsible for oneself?
By remembering to do your work. The system works if you use it. No one can remember for you. This is wonderful news because you then possess your own soul. Although we are each alone, we have each other and the outside help that is implied in a conscious school. Without one's self, there is nothing with which to adore the Absolute or assist in achieving his aims.

What does it mean to create one's self?
There is a soul in our bodies, and self-remembering has a cumulative effect; the soul grows stronger and it creates itself by adding to itself through being present. The soul is not mortal.

Truly, there is nothing to take from another, but there is something to find and give within oneself. It isn't so much a question of why I should remain an enigma to you, but rather why must you remain an enigma to yourself? One can only understand another to the extent one understands oneself.

Everything should be background to one's self. We have struck a deeper chord than life, and that is why we are here: to find our selves.

You will ultimately understand that the only thing that holds you back is yourself. To be true to oneself will always remain the oldest pursuit upon the earth; it was why the earth and man were created.

One's self is a phenomenon separate from the machine, yet shallow identifications attempt to interrupt the birth of higher centers.

By placing oneself last, one places one's self first.

There are many things about which one can do nothing. As Mr. Ouspensky noted, it is most unjust that we die, or that our machines must expire. Although we can do little about our death, we can do much for our astral body before the physical body perishes. The hidden function of one's machine is to create an immortal soul. The idea of transformation is buried so deep, by so many layers of artificial appliances, or buffers and distractions, that it is difficult to reach it.

The soul is composed of an imperishable substance that becomes permanent. Like the fragrance of a rose, we can't see it, but it is there. It is molecular. At birth, when the soul enters the physical body, spirit enters matter.

We rarely question where the soul is before birth, although we sometimes think about where it will go after death. Where is the soul before birth? Thirty years from now, we will be sitting around the table and someone there will be twenty years old. His soul is somewhere tonight; I would suggest in a divine state of rest called limbo. Asleep or awake, we are enshrouded in universal mysteries.

How much does the soul depend on the physical body?
The soul has to transform the suffering of the physical body in order to come into being. The soul will always remain the result of its experiences. Each phase of one's life offers challenges and new identifications that one has to transform. The worth of our physical body lies in that which it contains—the soul. Self-remembering is all we have, and even our bodies are only luggage that must be left by the roadside.

We do know enough to create souls, and that is a great deal. Assuredly, those who study methods to develop their souls are in a superior position to those who do not.

If we could increase our perception and understanding, then could we act in a particular way?

You would, perhaps, be closer to what you imagine is superior conduct. The soul is quite separate on this plane, and is undeniably itself. We would be lost if we could adequately describe our soul, if it were words rather than itself. Consciousness is not functions; our soul is not our brain, not our intellectual center.

One way to recognize the soul is to recognize what it is not. It is not negative emotions, and it is not one's chief feature. It's quite interesting to see your arm as an apparatus, a crane. When you see that, it is your soul looking at the machine objectively. When you are dividing attention, your soul is present.

We have an indescribable jewel in ourselves—our soul. Eastern schools called the soul a precious gem. It is not what speaks. It is a little soul in a vessel, what some teachings call "the nameless one."

History gathers all people, for anything we can see must inevitably perish. Thus, of the many miracles on this earth, the greatest by far is the creation of one's soul, as time will not deface it. There are many people in the teaching who would make the ultimate sacrifice to awaken. They would give their lives, if necessary, to create a soul.

We are seeing the best of one another tonight, and the part of one another that we especially love. Let us toast to your soul—it is there.

INFLUENCE C

Influence C is a sacred celestial influence coming to us from the stars and is not to be confused with terrestrial influences.

One does not know Influence C until one meets it, and then one verifies it through transforming suffering. It is a privilege to meet Influence C, but the experience is a painful one.

Influence C is just a clinical phrase for angels or gods. It is a phrase designed to escape our prejudices, one that we can relate to freshly. It is more appealing if we think of it as Celestial Influence. Influence C can sound like a rubber stamp, but Celestial Influence sounds divine.

In the Bible it is said, "Many are called, but few are chosen." The expression, "few are chosen," reveals that some intelligence is making the selection. Mr. Gurdjieff, Mr. Ouspensky and Mr. Collin referred to a higher mind arranging one's fate as "Conscious Influence." Man is not the highest power in the universe; indeed, he is almost powerless and is the real alien of the earth.

You must recognize what is within your power to verify. Man is such a vain creature that he thinks he can resolve the enigmas of the universe. In the past higher forces were known as angels or gods. Homer long ago said, "All men have need of the gods." That was true then and it is equally true now. You know that you are playing the role of your name, and that each day a script is written especially for your evolution. This much you can verify. Some concepts, however, you cannot verify. And yet, you can clearly understand that self-remembering is always better than sleep, that it is always right action.

Are gods the same as angels?
Yes. Angels, gods and conscious beings are synonymous. The reason the Fourth Way uses the term "higher forces"—or Influence C, Conscious Influence—is to allow for a new understanding of the concept and to eliminate pre-conceived notions.

During September, 1967, I met Influence C through my first teacher. I have never been so impressed with anything else. When Influence C revealed themselves to me, life after death instantly became a fact.

What does "Influence C" mean but angels? It is a word designed for our scientific age. Angels are incredible forces. Before we met the system and the school, we wondered if there was life after death, higher forces, or such things as angels or gods.

Influence C remains and I remain. Influence C ushers us to Heaven's gate. God's direct influence does not reach the earth, but his indirect influence reaches us through Influence C.

Does each of us have an angel assigned to us?
We underestimate how much work one conscious being is capable of achieving. If I told you, it would sound absurd, but one angel is capable of an enormous amount of work. They move at tremendous speeds. Man can fly at twice the speed of sound in airplanes and man is a creation of the angels. It is good not to be naïve and take things too personally. Basically, forty-four conscious beings spread their work throughout the school.

Higher forces help us every day. Sometimes they give us gifts (suffering) that are difficult to bear, but they are not punishing us.

One can see the direction in which Influence C wishes to move by what they are doing. I understand Influence C well. They are not negative, although they utilize weaknesses of ours such as feminine dominance. I cannot stress enough what a gift it is that higher forces have revealed themselves to us. They rarely reveal themselves, even to conscious beings. We receive Influence C because life rejects it. They pursue Influence A, while we pursue Influence C.

We each have a subjective machine with subjective vision. Influence C is assisting us, but the human machine cannot see metaphysical impressions. It can see the carnations, but it cannot see the fragrance of the carnations because it isn't designed to do so. The gods can perhaps see such things as wind currents, fragrances, and so on.

We are all equally mechanical, but things begin to get better when we meet Influence C. Once one has verified that higher forces do exist, one does not deserve their assistance if one questions their methods. Indeed, they release one if one spends too much time asking "why" instead of "how."

It is difficult to ask Influence C for help, because the help one receives is suffering that one is expected to transform.

With Influence C one has to think of reverses and opposites, twists and turns, a great sense of humor along with profound tragedy. They are complete masters of the unpredictable.

Awakening has to be difficult or we wouldn't want it, and it is completely impossible to achieve without Influence C. Higher forces have pushed us many times to the brink, but not over it. They can make a heaven or hell out of any environment.

It is interesting that higher forces assist us, isn't it? And the most we can do for them is to transform suffering rather than resent it, because nothing physical is of use to them—they are metaphysical. They help us out of their love for us and for humanity.

How rarefied is the knowledge that we share—we almost take it as fact to see the work of the gods. It is quite rare, and almost all conscious beings are kept naïve due to the nature of their task. No matter how much we know, we are still reduced to hope and faith—hope that Influence C will place our souls in limbo and send them back again into a conscious role. This may be a fact for Influence C, but it remains a theory for us; even so, everything points to the reality of it.

Every second we remember ourselves is ours throughout eternity. Higher forces have created our physical bodies, and after the body perishes, they have methods of preserving the immortal moments produced by our soul during life upon the earth.

The older one becomes, the more one appreciates Influence C. There is much for us to understand, and each of us must understand the aims of Influence C personally. The school is a factory to produce individual souls.

Change is truly the only permanent characteristic we have. It is impossible not to change with Influence C helping us, and that is why we are here, to become like them. It is not so much a question of whether the teacher exists or whether Influence C exists, but whether *you* exist.

To touch Influence C one must transform suffering. Influence C does not desert one. People don't control their own destiny; it is in the hands of Influence C.

Is our ability to remember ourselves controlled by the gods?
Yes. One is paced through nine lifetimes, and each life is all that one can bear. Each person who enters the way will become immortal—that is why the way exists. The life of each person who

enters the way is an epic, yet how many lives we live in this one lifetime. Sometimes one remembers with relief that higher forces are monitoring the school. We have the great privilege of understanding that higher forces do exist, and that life after death is a reality. Where does the way lead to? Immortality.

Mr. Ouspensky once said to Rodney Collin that one must do everything one can, and then he simply raised his finger, pointing to Influence C. There are great works of art that picture an upraised finger pointing to higher forces. It was a favorite motif of Leonardo da Vinci, one that he used in his *St. John.*

What we seek is eternal and is quite independent of the age we live in.

Since angels can manage anything necessary on earth, God's direct influence does not reach us. Sometimes we can glimpse the intelligence of angels when, for example, we understand that they invented the microcosmos man, who can transcend himself and create an astral body. Intellectual parts of centers are a treasure that they conceived. Angels thrive on being externally considerate—it is a permanent state for them. We are stones that they have brought to life and, although we are essentially children, considerable results are expected of us.

We have the highest religion possible: angels working openly to help us create our astral bodies. Our prayers have been answered; now we must endure.

The sooner one bends, the better. If we could understand Influence C we would be angels. There is nothing they will not do to produce awakening. We are the fortunate recipients of their work.

We have tonight and Influence C—we can verify this much. The aim of the school is to create souls, but there is not simply one aim. Many things are true and are occurring simultaneously.

Our fate is tightly sealed, and it is excellent. We have been chosen by Influence C to awaken, while almost all others have an indifferent fate. That is, they are left alone to a great extent by higher forces. Influence C wants something for us: an astral body. And they want something from us: an ark to survive hydrogen warfare.

We could not evolve without friction. We aren't meant to identify with shocks, but to produce the third state of consciousness by transforming them. There is nothing we cannot survive—what choice is there?

Higher forces would be ashamed of the way they treat us if they didn't know they were creating immortal souls. They have a terrible job. Strange, isn't it, that they give us their work? There are gods in the room right now. We cannot see them with our physical eyes, but they are here, much as the fragrance of the rose is here. We must take the same road that they took: the road of transforming suffering.

It is painful to have friends leave the school.
Sadness is a noble emotion, yet transforming it is a higher alternative. Things could always be much worse. It is far better to utilize shocks than to resist them, and eventually one learns not to quarrel with Influence C. To a large extent, I've simply accepted their methods because I know that questioning them won't change them. People who lose Influence C destroy themselves. Their departure is a loss, but identifying with their departure is a greater loss. That is not self-remembering, but feminine dominance.

Influence B is for people content with relative awakening, while Influence C is for people who wish to awaken fully. No one puts enough pressure on themselves, which is one of the reasons

Influence C provides shocks. We have to undergo terrible suffering because man is created in God's image, and God had to suffer unspeakably to create his astral body.

As one verifies Influence C, one's own thoughts become more terrible. Influence C puts thoughts into our minds to awaken the ruling faculty. It's a great relief to understand that one is not one's many 'I's. A student asked me, "How does one verify Influence C?" I advised him that a series of events will occur that are too numerous to be ascribed to chance.

Higher forces test one in a variety of ways to see if one is worthy, and all one must do is value them above everything else. You have established a tie with the unknown, yet Influence C will do everything they can to shake you off, to see if you are worthy of them. We all need the same things to awaken—attention from them, which means transforming friction.

Mr. Ouspensky said that God did not create man, but assigned to higher school the task of creating a self-evolving being. We are a simple little school on earth, and we have a tie to higher school, Influence C. We represent a growing end of the Ray of Creation, and we enable Influence C to go on to even higher levels by eventually taking their place.

One needs to utilize the unexpected; one hardly can use the expected. Shocks anticipated too correctly cease to be shocks. Expect the unexpected—who knows what is going to occur tonight or tomorrow?

Hydrogen warfare seems inevitable, and one no longer has to be a prophet to predict it. Incredible events may happen in our lives, and I will be very surprised if anything but us survives. We are not better than anyone, but we are luckier than everyone.

Influence C has been working with me for almost twenty-five years, and there are perhaps forty more years to come. Some of us will experience fifty to eighty years of Influence C. I have spent these years doing my best to speak creatively about one word—self-remembering—and never expecting a greater idea from Influence C, because that is our all and everything. Some people want something else, but they will never get anything better.

I've learned to trust Influence C even though they've sent me into dead-end streets to receive rough handling. At first one comes away staggering and stunned. Influence C is serious about the work. They will not overlook what each person needs, and they know how to reduce one's false personality. They use crushing methods. Everyone suffers with or without the system, but we have the opportunity to transform suffering. Compared to Influence C, our strength is hardly that of a sparrow.

We have encountered the miraculous—Influence C. We are people who have consumed our youth in producing magnetic centers in order to find Influence C. But people in life have consumed their youth with nothing to show for it. We have Influence C to show for it. We really can't give Influence C anything except the transformation of suffering, which they expect as well as our love.

It is startling that man is worthy to share in the Ray of Creation. When one is remembering oneself, one is a different order of creation. I marvel that we can speak words like this. With self-remembering one is leading something other than a biological existence—one is becoming conscious. Without self-remembering one is like a man number one, two or three. It's hard to realize that there are five to six billion people on the earth tonight, and Influence C has selected us to evolve.

No achievement of ours is as great as establishing a connection with Influence C. Next to that anything is almost nothing.

Angels will do all they can to awaken us—nothing keeps Influence C from actualizing their aim. Behind sleep, the stars; behind awakening, the gods.

We do have the immeasurably good fortune of establishing a connection with Influence C, and this is a great comfort, insofar as one can be consoled in such a monumental struggle as awakening. Influence C are very pleased to give the gift of awakening, but they are frugal with it, and give it to only a few. We must always take what C Influence give us and be grateful for it, whatever it is.

There is a line to heaven that is millenia long, and yet we are at the head of the line. Influence C wish to give their gifts to someone and, through inexplicable luck, we have been chosen.

Rainer Maria Rilke said, "All angels bring terror"—terrible shocks to awaken one. To create an astral body they use unsavory methods. Influence C frequently plays the role of villain in our lives. With them, one just absorbs continually; it is the highest path. One tries to endure without self-pity. It is curious, but Influence C crushes us into immortality.

What does Rilke mean when he speaks about impressing angels?
That means to be in essence, be yourself, transform negative emotions. One should not want to impress anyone. One can hardly impress angels since they created us and we are their offspring.

There is not one word I say that is not monitored by higher forces—the play is that complete, and it is written by them. The people who speak and the words they speak are all fated. This does not diminish the play, however. If one does not know what Influence C wish, one can try to remember oneself. They wish that.

One cannot wonder at one's ignorance sufficiently.

Ours is an objective religion. That is, men can become gods by remembering themselves and transforming suffering.

Influence C is almost totally responsible for creating the third state in us. Whether the third state arrives through one's own efforts, the efforts of friends, or Influence C, one should be grateful.

The real battle is not with another person or event, it is with one's own mind activity, the many 'I's. There is really only one significant issue: to be or not to be present. Often, all Influence C wish is for one to be present. The Absolute went through barriers, which has enabled the rest of us sparrows to pass through.

Mr. Gurdjieff said the Absolute's influence does not reach us directly, and he is correct. Influence C help us. We do not need God—the Absolute—he is too big for us and has more important matters to attend to. Influence C are capable of meeting our needs.

Homer said, "The gods do not make themselves known to all men." Influence C do not let many people find them as we have. They don't want awakening to become common because that would cheapen awakening and reduce the Absolute, who struggled unspeakably to create his astral body. Many students have verified that an invisible conscious influence is working with them. It is difficult to conceive that higher forces would invest such an enormous amount of work in the role of each person who enters the way and then simply discard their efforts later.

To understand higher school is a challenge because the level of being of Influence C is so much greater than our own. We work with many theories that are facts for higher school. Whatever we cannot verify we must neutrally record rather than accept or reject. We have received Celestial Influence, which is immeasurably different from any earthly influence, but life will never notice it. Influence C have already proven themselves; it is we who must prove ourselves.

Verifying Influence C is not a gentle process—one becomes haggard. Young or old, man or woman, Influence C gives to all the friction needed to evolve. They always have something problematic waiting for us, something that will need to be transformed.

When one first enters the way, it seems as if one were chosen from life but, as one sees more clearly, one realizes that one's role was created before one was born. Center of gravity and alchemy are important variables that cannot be left to chance and still produce the right result.

At the conclusion of his earthly life Mr. Ouspensky, who had once sought the miraculous, *became* the miraculous. His devoted fellow conscious spirit, Rodney Collin, wrote of his end, and his beginning, in *The Theory of Eternal Life:* "Of my own teacher I can only say that he also produced among his friends a play, of which they unwittingly but perfectly played their part, and whose plot was his own death. Silent, he instructed them in their hearts, some recognizing and some not. 'I will always be with you,' he too could say—but lightly and smoking a cigarette, so that none noticed. Lying in bed in Surrey, he possessed with his own mind a young man flying over the Atlantic, whom he had already rid of an illusion. That morning, dead, he walked with a traveller—crossing London Bridge, and to another at the wheel of a car showed the nature of the universe. Yet these tales are hard to believe. Of his achievement, then, let this present book stand witness, written this year following his death, of knowledge undeserved by me. Let him who can understand, understand. For so it is."

If people who enter the way become immortal, where is the idea of chance?
The Fourth Way is for people who know too much. If we knew what Influence C knows we would heave a sigh of a relief, because to my knowledge those entering the way cannot miss becoming immortal. People who enter the way have truth, divine destiny.

Christ said, "Straight is the way that leadeth unto life and few there be that find it." What seems like our chance meeting with Influence C is in reality the destiny of our eternal good fortune.

Is nothing sacred to Influence C?
Nothing but your aim to awaken.

All significant achievements on the earth are monitored by Influence C. We are truly involved in tremendous events, such as hydrogen warfare, and yet these events favor us because they have evoked a school on earth from higher forces. This school enables you to escape.

ART

Our specialty is self-remembering. Nothing approaches it, not even the arts.

An accomplished artist may have developed controlled attention in all four centers without having cultivated the art of self-remembering. Divided attention is school work—it is a hidden idea, designed for only a few people. Regardless of how large our school becomes, we must remember that we represent an infinitesimal portion of humanity.

We appreciate the arts and have a limited understanding of them, but what we really understand is divided attention—how to create a soul.

It is wonderful that we are professional with self-remembering. It is our "field." The arts are very beautiful, but they are a distant second to one's self, one's own divinity. Throughout history, only a few have viewed the world's beautiful objects of art with divided attention. It is interesting that music does not endure, but what listens to it—with divided attention—lasts forever. In this way music serves us.

Our school is learning to value art, but the transformation of suffering is our main sustenance. Fortunately, not only the transformation of suffering, but also the transformation of impressions generates energy for self-remembering. Art civilizes and inspires one's soul. Being present while experiencing the arts is a remarkable way to evolve since the more we become, the more we see and hear.

There are many tempting deviations, and art is one of them. We are not supposed to get identified with art. Identification is like flypaper—try not to get one finger caught in it, or two fingers, or ten fingers. I do enjoy all of the arts, but I'm also distracted by them. There are so many things to take our attention. We have the good fortune to have correct scale and relativity about the arts. One has to look at an enormous number of pictures and visit many museums in order to establish this scale. We have such good luck here because we live for the present, we keep art in perspective and we keep it from becoming a noble buffer.

One must learn to discern a fine painting from a poor one. One cannot rely upon reputation alone. This is a major point: one must know for oneself what is of value, and one cannot know this unless one has the strength of being behind one's observations.

It is necessary to increase one's knowledge of art, music and literature. One needs to remember the scale of this education, however, because it doesn't approach the significance of self-remembering. I try to prevent students from being taken in by their art form—our specialty is self-remembering. Many students try to become proficient in the arts, but they also need to see the relative place of art in their work. Our self is our most important possession. When you listen to music or look at paintings, try to use these art forms to divide attention and civilize your soul. Try to avoid "either or" thinking when pondering self-remembering and art. There is a place for both and each makes the other better.

Music can create the remarkable sense of urgency that self-remembering requires. Consciousness is unforgiving, and higher centers will not allow themselves to be penetrated by anything other than self-remembering.

The arts are a divine mirror of nature, and they attract us because they both reflect and rise above nature.

How can we prolong and make the work exciting?
By being receptive to impressions, the arts, nature; best of all, to one another. The arts are so much better than being preoccupied with uninteresting mind activity, and they give one something to be present to. They give our school a direction.

We are being educated in the arts so that we may preserve the best of mankind for the future of mankind. With self-remembering, one can pursue one's self *and* one's art, and do both better. Art, if it is true to itself, must always point to something beyond itself. One's soul, friendship and art are old companions. First of these is one's soul, then friendship, then the arts. The three mutually fortify one another.

Why do we collect art?
Beauty produces its likeness in those who pursue it. This wonderful system stresses raising the level of impressions around one. Our school invests in art to strengthen the impressions octave.

We talk about culture a fair amount, but its highest achievement is to lead to self-remembering. It is a bridge, and many bridges lead to higher centers. When we speak about art, we must remember it is a distant second to self-remembering and we must use it as a medium to divide attention. Johann Goethe said about looking at art, "In the end we return to a wordless beholding."

When I look at art, I usually try to look without words. Sometimes the intellectual center gets in the way and talks about art instead of experiencing it. This is similar to talking about self-remembering instead of experiencing self-remembering. When we are speaking about art, try not to let self-remembering disappear behind the subject, because art fulfills its highest purpose when it is accompanied by self-remembering. One uses it rather than being used by it.

We appreciate art because we recognize that sex energy has been usefully directed, but people who are involved in art have deviated from the highest use of sex energy by pursuing the arts rather than higher centers.

Art is no substitute for self-remembering, but the soul does need something with which to nourish its essence. Socrates said, "All men are in a state of spiritual and physical gestation and need an environment of beauty in which to nurture their birth." However, expression in art is a dead end without self-remembering.

It helps to have an interest in the arts, because it enables students to hold on to the school. Conscious beings are often artists.

Objective art is appealing in any age, but art can only take one to the threshold of one's soul. True art is founded upon transforming suffering, and a true artist is a world unto himself. Art is synonymous with one's self and there is no higher art form than one's own individual soul.

You cannot touch great art unless you transform great suffering.

THE FOURTH WAY

The system is the oldest civilized heritage on this earth. When one enters the way, one has established a connection with the conscious aspects of the Ray of Creation found on earth. Regardless of when one appears on this earth, the critical questions always concern man and the universe. That is, man the machine, and higher centers awakening within it.

Men leave the work, but the work does not leave man.

I do not imagine that there has ever been a way or path to the truth that was not strange, because one is taking a machine at a physical level and transforming it into an astral body. I would not teach or use my energy unless I felt that immortality was probable and that death was an illusion for those who enter the way.

When one meets a system, the residue of one's magnetic center serves as denying force for one's steward. Most systems in the world are at least partially true and, as vehicles for conscious influence, they may have allowed some to escape. One should be wise enough, however, to concentrate upon this system through which the life of consciousness is breathing now.

Life is difficult with or without the system. You know how difficult it is to be awake *with* this system; without it, people are totally asleep.

How important is it to be a success in life?
It is useful to be a good businessman, a good householder. The Fourth Way occurs in life, and eighty-five percent of our school is in life. Being successful in life enables one to travel and to educate one's essence.

A good householder is characterized by his awareness of the esoteric, which distinguishes him from a person who simply is well-groomed and maintains orderly surroundings. Furthermore, a good householder uses objective ideas and common sense to approach daily situations. He regards controlling his centers as his first priority, and he pursues his self above all things because he understands that without self-remembering, he is not. Entering the way requires the exceptional sense of values intrinsic to a good householder.

How can one work with 'I's that think one is not able to maintain the pace of the school?
If you value self-remembering and the school above everything else, you won't have any problem keeping pace; be true to yourself and everything will fall into place.

It is easier to misunderstand the system than to understand it, yet the system unravels the essential mysteries. The system is so profound that it does not leave one simply with a workable vocabulary—it releases one from it. It is equivalent to a hand pointing toward higher realms. It points to *you*, and you are not a word. You are a state, when you can attain it.

The Fourth Way removes symbols of identity and gives one identity itself. A conscious teaching can be a temporary symbol of identity for one, and yet the system is so great that it works to minimize even that weakness. The Fourth Way leaves nothing for one to rely upon but reality.

The Fourth Way dispenses with rituals, and yet one's whole life becomes the noble art of remembering oneself. We do not speak about self-remembering all the time, and yet we are all trying to remember ourselves, which is an example of transcending the system. Speaking about self-remembering is practicing instead of performing. If one does not go beyond the system it becomes dogma. Mr. Ouspensky said that all the ideas of the system are subordinate to, and revolve around, self-remembering. Never expect the system to offer anything more valuable than self-remembering—that is more than enough.

The system *does* work: that is, people do produce souls through it.

The system itself can be a buffer when our machines endeavor to make the school look poor by making extreme efforts. False personality cajoles one into thinking that the work is responsible for one's difficulties. The Fourth Way is infallible; it is one's own weaknesses that account for failures.

Mr. Ouspensky said the Fourth Way cannot be popular because of its negative character—it doesn't flatter man's position. People need symbols of identity for a while: movements, word exercises and so on. The Fourth Way carefully removes these symbols and forces one back on oneself, exactly where one belongs. We begin as Renoir's *Bohemian*, and end as El Greco's *Tears of St. Peter*—on our knees.

Mr. Ouspensky's *In Search of the Miraculous* is so far above the level of life that it passes by unnoticed.

Awakening is mathematical, but if the teaching is presented with too much precision, it sterilizes the work.

One is on the way when one fits one's life into the teaching rather than fitting the teaching into one's life. Also, one is on the way when one personally knows that there is nothing to turn back to.

One has entered the way when intervals cease to be a deterrent to remembering oneself. Mr. Ouspensky said that one may have everything, but if one does not have the luck to be chosen to enter the way, one has nothing.

The Fourth Way wouldn't work if people didn't learn and pass it on. When one enters the way, one verifies the hidden meaning of life in the universe. No one who has entered the way will trade anything for his evolutionary position within the school.

Transforming suffering becomes a way of life when one enters the way. Once one is on the way, one all but dies during one's evolution. It is tacitly understood that all people who enter the way have difficult roles to enact.

When one enters the way there are fewer questions, because one has learned to value the idea of self-remembering; one understands that what one seeks is a state and not a question.

One can be said to be on the way when one understands for oneself that there is nothing else for one. Many people know how to seek, but few know how to find. Seeking is often a buffer for a person with a magnetic center, because actually beginning the epic struggle to awaken can be too formidable. Without efforts one is mired in allurement.

The system offers the theory that one cannot enter the way until another person is placed upon one's ladder. When one enters the way one attracts a replacement with a like valuation for awakening. People on the same ladder will have similar characteristics.

How does one know if one is on the way?
Time is a factor. As the years pass, if one has been within the school ten, fifteen years, that is a verification. Mr. Ouspensky said, "Schools are for people who need schools, and who know they

need them." If one does not know that one needs a school, then, of course, one has lost the way.

Is it possible to be in the school and not be on the way?
Yes. A small percentage of the people who meet the school enter the way. Everyone who enters the way in our school is worked with openly by Influence C. Homer said that the gods do not reveal themselves to all men. In fact, they do not reveal themselves to many, but they do reveal themselves to those on the way in our school. The system deals with many facts but, to keep it from becoming dogmatic, they are presented as theories.

The system can only benefit one if one uses it. It isn't how much time one spends with the system that is important, but rather how one uses one's time in the system.

The system works because it produces results, results are proportionate to efforts. The Fourth Way encourages one not to show what one has gained. If one exhibits what one has gained, what could be the source of this display other than false personality? One's self is metaphysical, and it can shine forth lucidly for three minutes or three seconds. And this is *you*.

MAN NUMBER FOUR

A true man number four is the product of a school. His main desire, which dominates all others, is to awaken. If he were perfect or consistent he would be a complete man number seven, because unity is a property of a man number seven. A man number four is responsible for being true to his aim to awaken.

All of human history has been characterized by warfare; Plato said that war is a permanent state for humanity. Men number one, two and three exist for the moon and the earth, while man number four exists for himself. The development of consciousness is the hidden meaning of life for man.

A man number four vacillates between the heaven of self-remembering and the hell of sleep, and his failures outnumber his successes, but not indefinitely. If you have a right attitude toward failures, and if you don't identify with them by becoming disappointed, something marvelous can occur: each time you fail, you remember yourself.

It is humiliating for a man number four to be governed by transient 'I's. At an early stage, man number four does not observe this process, but a mature four can sometimes sever associative thinking.

Man number four is often given blunt shocks because subtle shocks pass by unnoticed. A man number four learns early to make the most of today's pleasures if he is to enjoy his life. Shocks rapidly follow one another, and if one prolongs the initial shock in a state of self-pity or resentment, the next shock overlaps.

What does it mean to be a man number four?
A permanent aim to awaken. A man number four is a product of a conscious school and is on the way. Furthermore, a man number four desires transforming suffering above sleep.

One meets a Fourth Way school through one's magnetic center—one is magnetically attracted to a conscious teaching. Quickly one develops an observing 'I', which can be one or a small group of 'I's. Deputy steward is a further growth of observing 'I' and possesses a greater ability to observe and photograph mechanical manifestations. Yet deputy steward is basically powerless to control what it observes, because it is weakened by the mechanical 'I's. When one enters the way one develops, to varying degrees, a steward whose capacity to observe and regulate the four lower functions is superior to that of deputy steward. Controlling centers is reserved for one's self, as one wishes one's master, and not one's steward, to ascend. Furthermore, when one possesses a steward one has progressed from true personality—World 48—to essence—World 24—and one has also accumulated a series of third state experiences. Yet higher centers do manifest without awareness in a man number four, as Worlds 12 and 6 are embryonic. A baby is not aware of its first attempts to walk, and one's self begins from such a simple position.

Our machine is always discontent with self-remembering because it is not mechanical.

A man number four is apt to disintegrate into different personalities. Generally, a man number four surveys the parts and has difficulty grasping the whole.

It is useful to remember that no state is permanent for a man number four, not even self-remembering. The less favored states pass and, unfortunately, the more favored ones do also. This is why standards are necessary, as they prevent one from descending below them.

How can one remember small aims?
Man number four is subject to forgetfulness because higher centers are not permanently functioning within him. When he first heard of the concept of self-remembering and tried to practice it, Mr. Ouspensky, like the rest of us, discovered that he could not remember himself. Most people are incapable of such a sincere observation. If one's aims are connected with self-remembering, one's activities will not pose a problem.

It is enormously difficult for a man number four to remember himself even three seconds after establishing a small aim to do so because the struggle is always of the second.

A man number four must relinquish mechanical control in order to gain conscious control. Time is a necessary element in this process, as it is difficult to see certain functions as mechanical which have served one well. Yet buffers must be abandoned to permit the emergence of one's true self.

There are four basic centers of gravity in human machines: the instinctive, the moving, the emotional and the intellectual. It is difficult for one center of gravity to manifest as another would, because each brain prefers to exist for itself. The intellectual center does not wish to be emotional, nor does the emotional center strive to be intellectual. When a man number four balances all four centers, emotionality penetrates the machine regardless of center of gravity. Authentic emotions are hard to bear. Nevertheless, a man number five must endure intense states in order for higher centers to develop within him.

Do one's center of gravity, alchemy and other mechanical factors become more illusory as one evolves?

They cease to be the issue. Consciousness is not functions, and self-remembering proceeds, apart from them. Eventually one uses common sense and utilizes the advantages they offer.

When a highly emotional state is produced, a buffer of dullness enters. How may one eliminate this interruption?

For a man number four, an intense emotional experience is a result of one's king of hearts and higher centers being activated. If dull feelings occur, the intellectual part of one's emotional center has descended and the emotional part has ascended through the negative expression of boredom or indifference. The study of functions is a major aim to pose for oneself, since it requires years to verify the existence of each center within one's machine. I once had a former student who said he was a man number five. I told him, "That is not self-remembering. Try to be present and let the numbers take care of themselves. It is very difficult to be a man number four." Try to maintain standards.

How can a man number four determine if right efforts are being made?

Time is a factor in distinguishing a right from a wrong effort. One shouldn't expect perfection, as transforming failure produces the inner friction necessary for awakening. Additionally, one needs to accumulate varied experiences. This is possible within the school as higher forces design situations in which students learn to discriminate between productive and fruitless efforts. Such situations are difficult to endure because they include powerful shocks, for which one is often unprepared. Shocks must be alarming to awaken one, and they can produce an intense electrical experience that thrusts World 12 or World 6 into being.

Distrust is not altogether a negative phenomenon, because the intellectual part of the emotional center must discriminate to know right from wrong action. One should not dwell upon distrust, however, as it can quickly become a negative emotion, and one can become subject to paranoia. One must trust Influence C, especially when things are difficult.

Men number four are in a desperate position whether they recognize it or not. Once one has discovered the concept of self-remembering one's time is limited because the system is no toy, and it shuns the insincere. We are a real school. A man number four inwardly searches for something he has forgotten during the day. Then, with alarm, he realizes that he has forgotten himself. Be grateful for being in essence, as it is a bridge to higher centers.

One of the greatest difficulties in awakening for a man number four is establishing scale correctly. Work on being must proceed in simple, commonplace situations, since major shocks come our way less frequently than opportunities to make small efforts, which are available to us daily. One cannot discriminate unless one establishes scale, and one cannot establish scale without transforming suffering. A weakness in scale means that one does not know which among many fragments of knowledge carries the most mass; one must be careful not to consider all the knowledge on the same level. Another major weakness of a man number four is the inability to establish relativity. A weakness in relativity indicates that one does not know when to apply the appropriate, relative thought to a situation.

One must realize that one is not consistent. A characteristic of a man number four is inconsistency, since experiencing fluctuations is a law of awakening. Because one of the major enemies of a man number four is inconsistency, it is an immense challenge to try to be one person. On a given day seven people are elevated and three are low. Mr. Ouspensky said that reliability distinguishes one student from another.

On a certain scale self-pity is a legitimate emotion for a man number four, but Mr. Ouspensky said that the facts lie. One must assimilate friction properly to not indulge in self-pity. Make the right choice and choose self-remembering over self-pity.

A man number four needs to be careful of losing energy over his future fate. Make efforts and accept results.

A man number four requires the assistance of a steward in his work. A steward emulates higher centers while understanding that it is designed to serve one's master, a state without words. One's steward employs words such as, "Do not become fascinated with what you are observing," and, "Be present to the music." Men number four are often infatuated with manipulating outward forms; consciousness, however, is not functions.

A man number four is naïve to the scale of the aim that he is posing for himself—it is incredibly difficult to escape death. Yet there is a tendency in a man number four to consider his efforts sufficient. Jesus wore a crown of thorns to symbolize that transforming suffering is the method through which one's higher centers come into being. It is arduous to persist beyond one's capacities, yet that is what awakening requires. Conversely, if one produces minimal efforts, degeneration ensues.

I find work on negative emotions the most difficult part of the system. Do you still experience negativity?
Mr. Ouspensky said that in the octave of awakening, self-remembering was the mi-fa interval, and transforming suffering the si-do interval. It is unspeakably difficult because it is not mechanical. I still have considerable difficulty transforming negative emotions, primarily due to the violence of the suffering I must absorb to lift a school and humanity out of the chaos of impending hydrogen warfare.

A man number five's center of gravity is in the transformation of negative emotions into positive ones. When a man number four transforms negative emotions, he experiences some of the qualities of a man number five. In certain moments, a mature man number four is a man number five but, although he can briefly experience the being of a man number five, he cannot sustain it. He usually manifests the conduct of a man number four and, without trying to self-remember, he differs little from life. If a man number four could sustain the non-expression of negative emotions, he would not be a number four, he would be a man number five. Every man number four who enters the way will be given what he needs.

Self-remembering has become an old refrain that we keep returning to: the fog of imagination, then presence; fog, presence. The discipline to separate from the disappointment of forgetting oneself is a necessary self-defense for a man number four.

Men number one, two and three are oblivious to the planets and to themselves. Mr. Ouspensky stated that in the world of men number one, two and three, will is the "resultant of desires." If one enters the way, one must continue to resist mechanicality one's entire life and remember to strive for the right thing: to be present.

A man number four is a different order of creation than a man number one, two or three. One is different when one is remembering oneself, or transforming suffering, or not expressing negative emotions. Unlike men number one, two and three, we have self-remembering. Men number one, two and three are asleep in the name of God. Paul wrote, "They are asleep who are asleep in Christ's name."

What prevents a man number four from evolving further is unnecessary suffering. One needs large shocks to remind one that most of one's suffering is unnecessary.

There is no way for a man number four to be present other than a moment at a time. Be grateful for what you can gather each day, for nothing is as sweet as the present. Divided attention, when one can sustain it, is everything, and all else is nonsense.

It is in the nature of a man number four to sometimes distort reality, but life has almost completely distorted reality.

Realizing one's inability to remember oneself can be almost disabling. Perhaps the best way a number four can self-remember is to separate when he realizes he has not self-remembered.

Generally, self-remembering must originate in the emotional center for a man number four, because remembering oneself is an emotional experience. Also, one can control the emotional center if one does not express negativity, but this requires self-remembering. It is very hard for a man number four to relinquish unnecessary suffering, because it is a buffer to self-remembering.

To be a man number four is to be a soul in gestation, a soul that is evolving. Higher forces create bizarre shocks, sometimes brutal shocks, to produce higher centers in students; this is the nature of awakening, as we have received it, and we must accept Influence C on their terms.

Higher school sharing their knowledge with men number four is a labor of love, which we all welcome. Is not the harmony and order we have brought to our lives incredible? From nothing, we have established a relationship with the gods. Moments of self-remembering for a man number four are few, but eternal and precious.

It is important that a man number four *not* settle for the pace of another man number four. Men number four vary in their intensity and drive to awaken. Aristotle was asked, "How can we develop?" He said, "Press on those ahead and forget about those behind." The higher your level of being, the more true this is—you must not let others slow you down. However, in order to advance you also have to help others. Having done what you can you must continue at your own pace. As long as it furthers your aim to awaken, you should remain in a relationship. If it does not aid your evolution, then you should not continue the relationship. Each person must decide for himself. Awakening is a tumultuous process, and higher forces will use students as friction for each other whether one is married or single. A true relationship can only be successful if both people are living to be present.

Our false personalities may offer negativity to those with whom we feel close, because they know our weaknesses. We should externally consider most the people to whom we are the closest.

In a true relationship, which is a relatively rare phenomenon, people are together and yet apart. One needs to not intrude into the solitude of the other if it is a time for that person to be alone. A state of non-attachment is necessary.

No woman is worth the soul within a man and, conversely, no man is worth the soul within a woman.

Can a man number four experience love?
Yes. A man number four is part of the conscious aspects of the Ray of Creation. His love is partly conscious because he loves nothing more than his aim to awaken, which sometimes pushes him into the third state of consciousness.

One cannot possess consciousness and lack will or love. Lacking one, one lacks the others. One question to pose for yourself is, "What do I have?" You have your aim to remember yourself, which is your greatest pursuit. We can appreciate the quality of reliability in each other. If one is awake, one can love; if one is asleep, one cannot love.

The oldest test for man is woman, and the oldest test for woman is man. One must value one's self above anything outside oneself, although awakening and relationships do not preclude one another. Our chief buffers often have to do with the opposite sex. That is why conscious beings so often lose their wives. Influence C removes their greatest identification from them. Relationships can be a help or a hindrance; it depends upon the individual case. Essence is so tender and childlike. We each have a relationship with everyone else in this room.

The last entry in the *Gospel According to Thomas* speaks of the subject of women evolving. "Peter said to Jesus: Let Mary Magdalene go out from among us because women are not worthy of the life [higher centers]. Jesus said: See, I shall lead her, so that I will make her male [develop intellectual parts of centers and World 6 within her] that she too may become a living spirit resembling you males. For every woman who makes herself male will enter the kingdom of heaven." Conversely, every man who makes himself female (World 12) shall become conscious.

It is important for a man number four to realize that there is an inner and an outer circle. Be sure you aren't slowed down by others. Something I've tried to stress to students is not to go at another's pace, and not to go at a collective pace. Everyone gambles here, and there is just one issue: "To be or not to be."

Humanity was invented for a few to escape, and for the rest to be a part of the food chain.

One of the differences between a man number four and a man number five is that a man number five has an acute awareness of background sounds and activity, which is a characteristic of the functioning of higher centers. Higher centers for a man number four and five are as a dim light in the distance. A man number six is more bent and humble than a man number four or five.

You all do very well just to hear me. It is the discrepancy between a man number four and a man number seven, the discrepancy between your understanding and mine.

How can one minimize the feeling of uncertainty that intrudes upon one's moments of self-remembering?
This, too, is not self-remembering. You have nothing to lose. When you journey into unknown spheres, you are sacrificing the illusion of reality. Often the queen of hearts will ascend and reduce self-remembering by identifying with the things that surround one. Hermann Hesse, who was not a conscious being, wrote, "Safe in some accustomed sphere, we become lax. Our spirit wishes not to fetter us. Courage, my heart. Take leave, and fare thee well." Fortunately, I am a guide who has penetrated into and exists within the fourth dimension. You are following. Remember, what one gains, we all gain.

A man number four needs to be wary of thinking he has something because, when he compares himself with a man number one, two or three, he does have something. He has relative awakening. But relative awakening is not sufficient; full awakening is our aim and it is a realizable aim. I wouldn't make the effort to teach if it were not possible.

SCHOOL

Entering a school is the most important decision one makes in one's life, and it can be said that life begins when one meets a school. At that moment, self-remembering begins to emerge and mechanicality begins to fade.

The greatest requirement of school is for each person to be true to himself. To do this, one must sacrifice the irrelevant.

Many people seek us and, although we are doing everything we can to make ourselves available, it is still difficult to find us. The type of knowledge that we work with in this school is rarely experienced on the earth, as it maintains that the lives of men number one, two and three are tragedies. Life is a tragedy without the system, because there *is* no life without it.

We are becoming immortal. One's seconds of self-remembering may be meager, but they are one's own. The bookmarks used by the school are an invitation to immortality. I never hesitated to use them because Mr. Ouspensky met Mr. Gurdjieff through a newspaper advertisement.

The school is always in need of refinement. Mr. Ouspensky taught *why* we need to awaken. Our school teaches *how*, which is the difference between a theory and a real, practical school.

Mr. Ouspensky said it is the duty of a school to spread its influence as much as possible. The school has gone to great lengths to receive students. We presently have a network of sixty-five centers spread around the earth.

Even the aims of the school are secondary to being present because everything is nonsense compared to one's self. Focus without words; try not to identify; forget about events; try to be present.

We are all guests in this teaching, and we should not expect to establish the rules of awakening.

In our lifetime we have seen presidents and popes shot. Popes are the religious cells of the body of humanity, while presidents are the political cells. Our school represents the soul of humanity, its pineal activity.

Is it not surprising how few people there are to speak with about the system? Few are interested in hearing about the opportunity to develop a mature soul, because they think that they already have one. It doesn't speak well for humanity that it cannot see through the relatively shallow masks of Influences A and B.

One remarkable aspect of our school is that although it is occurring in an age of mass production, it is the most specific in its interpretation of awakening. In the midst of five to six billion people on the earth, we have hit the nail on the head.

Meetings are a third force in one's day. One attempts to be present as best one can, and yet various empty events distract one's being and become a denying force. Our collective energies, which are positive, are a third force to our efforts to be present.

Mr. Gurdjieff said that schools always make a profit. There is no event that one can't turn to one's advantage and transform if one has the right attitude toward denying force.

How can one work with 'I's that think one is not able to maintain the pace of the school?
Epictetus said, "Fate leads those who follow and drags those who resist." Influence C will help you realize your fate. "Be where you are, remember yourself" is a useful response to bring to such questions. One wants to help the school, and yet, after one has done everything one can, being present is the only way that one can help. Influence C is more interested in self-remembering than external achievements.

Our school functions because those who have entered the way have yielded their will to a higher will.

A monumental struggle to awaken is taking place within each student daily. A student of Mr. Ouspensky's said to him that although he had been with him for fifteen years he still had not experienced self-remembering. Mr. Ouspensky replied, "Have you truly been working for fifteen years, or have you just occupied a place here?"

While the school will take care of the students, it is more true that students must take care of the school. It is necessary to work for a greater aim than oneself throughout one's life—to assist the conscious aspects of the Ray of Creation.

There are many paths to truth. As we review history, we can see schools in many forms. As one begins to awaken, it is one's duty to help others, just as one has been helped. No school in history has stressed self-remembering to the extent that we have. Until this century the phrases, "self-remembering" or "remember yourself" were unknown. Mr. Gurdjieff, Mr. Ouspensky and Mr. Collin are conscious beings, but they did not create schools because of war and political instability; we have created a school where one can enter the way to become conscious.

A school is designed for people who are capable of crystallizing correctly. The reasoning faculty is faulty in those who are incapable of entering the way, because a faulty mind will make the truth a lie and the lie a truth. Lycurgus, the ninth-century B.C. law-giver, said, "When falls on man the wrath of the gods, first from his mind they banish understanding, and make the better judgment seem the worse, so that he may not know wherein he errs."

Our school will produce seven conscious beings. Apollo will not reach its peak for centuries or millennia. Our school is one of the greatest schools in recorded history, and that is why suffering is so abundant.

One must not stay in the same relationship to the ideas of the school, but keep pace with the new knowledge and new being that the school creates. A conscious teaching transforms itself many times in its history.

Can a school fail if collected effort is not enough?
Schools are designed to bridge, not fail, intervals.

If people understood the aims of the school better, would they understand efforts better?
Yes. Some people understand the needs of the school now, while others will realize them in two years, still others in ten years.

A school cannot exist without friction. Isn't it odd how simple the truth is? Coming from life, we are accustomed to hearing lies, but the truth is simple and profound. One becomes quite grateful for all the suffering people experience within the school because they do their best to transform it into consciousness. Transforming suffering ennobles all.

Eventually, one teaches by becoming the words one speaks. The school and the system can only be effective if one is prepared to transcend them. Identification with the system is one of the last obstacles that higher forces remove from one, because if the system is rightly received, it disallows identification with itself.

Extending photographs to others in areas in which we ourselves are weak places a pressure on us to control the same features. Many students who think they are school material are not, and eventually they become former students. One can only observe features for a certain period of time before one is expected to control them. If one cannot control them, one is released by higher forces.

If self-remembering makes you happy, then you have found the right place; the only thing we all like in this school is self-remembering.

When one is in the school, is one under the law of fate?
Men number one, two and three are asleep and are doomed to eternal recurrence. Mr. Ouspensky said schools are for people who know too much. Men number four are connected to Influence C, and they are fated to become conscious eventually. We know for certain that man is asleep, that life after death is reality and that Influence C is helping us.

How does one manage to remain practical when one is experiencing the mystical?
There is nothing more practical than experiencing mystical states; they are the fruition of our daily efforts. When you are present, allow the state to circulate throughout your being.

What is certain is that we have this life, and that Influence C exists. Our parents will play their roles again, but we will play more difficult roles until we reach our ninth and final life and "shuffle off this mortal coil." These roles will remain, but different actors will play them.

In a school, there exists an inner circle and an outer circle. The people who meet the school naturally start at the outer circle, and they penetrate the inner circle just by the magic of wishing to be there. The inner circle is not a place. It is primarily based upon a high valuation for one's self and the school. But one cannot completely understand this system in one or two years and, as long as one can breathe, one will be learning from it.

It is true that a school proceeds at the pace of the fastest students, and it is also a law that the higher must serve the lower.

The fastest students are slow, and yet their valuation is great. Mr. Ouspensky remarked that we must remember we are embarking upon a long journey, and schools are not for irresponsible people. It is a wonderful experience to work with people who don't need to be convinced of the necessity to remember themselves and transform suffering.

A newer student can speak with an older student concerning the rules, aims and exercises of the school, and one must do one's best to follow them. One will always derive the greatest profit from mastering the exercises that one favors least. Some areas must be defined and others not, for it is not necessarily useful to have all situations specifically defined, as the school would become formatory. If the school ever makes sense, it will fail; as long as it does not make sense, it will succeed. In his later years, Johann Goethe said that one inevitably becomes reluctant to give advice, because one has seen the most judicious enterprises fail and the most absurd ones succeed. The school is, in some respects, an absurd undertaking that is succeeding. And though it is illogical and a target of derision for some, its divine character remains undiminished and is, for those who understand its true nature, a godsend. Remember Influence C is a celestial, not a terrestrial, influence.

The outer circle understands the need to work less than the inner circle does. There are many things I don't bother to explain, because there isn't time to explain everything. I also know I don't

have to explain most things to students of the inner circle, for they
have their own working relationship with Influence C and they
attempt to remember themselves. There could be no school if one
had to explain everything, if there were no inner circle. The inner
circle has to have a job, and their job is to become more responsible; they understand themselves and advance by explaining the
system.

*How can one recognize whether one is in the inner or outer circle of
the school?*
The primary requirement for entering the inner circle is the desire
to be there. In this respect, there is justice. In order to progress to
the inner circle, one must transform suffering. Mr. Ouspensky said
that the Fourth Way has the wonderful advantage of being an
experienced system and, because it is ancient, the techniques are
simple and effective. One advances in relation to one's ability to
eliminate illusions, which is necessary because death reduces one
to no illusions. If one can truly perceive the miraculous nature of
the school, one is either in the inner circle or approaching it. In
addition, a person who enters the way has placed everything of
value in his life secondary to his aim of awakening. All who enter
the way are a part of the inner circle.

One must remember that many are called, but few are chosen.
One is either fated to enter the way or one is not. Although we
support each other, the teaching is designed to encourage strength
in individual students. People must learn to stand alone, because
death is a singular experience.

Being a nice person is not enough; one also has to have luck, which
Mr. Ouspensky called the most important factor in awakening.
Losing a school marks the ultimate calamity of one's life. I do not
want to share my energy with people who are leaving; I prefer to
share my energy with those who want to be here. As one partner
may outgrow the other in a marriage, so the school outgrows some
of its students.

Will those leaving the school make the students who remain stronger?
Yes. It doesn't surprise me that so many have left, but that so many
remain, when one considers that the price is so high. Remember
you seek immortality, and one can hardly pay enough.

The school works—it is producing consciousness in its participants. We have to work about sixteen to eighteen hours a day
to do it. What one person gains within the school, all gain. The
greater the will of the teacher, the higher the will of the student.
These are all laws for those in a conscious school.

It does not matter whether a conscious teaching appears in the
East or the West as long as it is a conscious teaching. Ultimately
one realizes that the truth cannot be spoken, for it is not a word,
and this accounts for the minimal use of words by teachers.

It is imperative to develop a proper attitude toward one's teacher,
because a teacher is the bridge between school on earth and higher
school. The more a teacher works with necessary laws, the greater
are each person's chances of creating a soul. One must learn to use
a teacher well and avoid misusing him. To have a right attitude
toward one's teacher, one would need to develop a proper attitude
toward each moment. Furthermore, it is necessary to cultivate
respect toward oneself, other students and teachers in the school.

As one begins to work more efficiently, one balances the three lines
of work: work for oneself, work for others and work for the school.
One needs to observe one's relation to the three lines of work
periodically to ensure that one's position is relatively balanced, not
perfectly balanced. Awakening is indirect, as the variables of the
system are often so invisible and numerous that one cannot
properly record them, which is fortunate. It is necessary to balance
the three lines of work, as it ensures a certain protection. When
one meets a system one is expected to work primarily on the first
line of work. Work for oneself may consist of attempting to listen,

which is a major aim to pose since one's machine is so easily distracted by trying to be an active force oneself.

There are so many octaves to get involved with in the school, and they all have their place, but nothing compares to self-remembering. If we are working correctly, we can bring self-remembering to those octaves. That is the meaning of working in life. How absurd it is to think about anything but self-remembering, unless it is some productive third line of work. Identifying with third line of work, however, is only a higher form of sleep.

If one devotes too much of one's time and energy to the first line of work at the expense of the other two lines, one's work has become selfish. In right order, first line of work leads to second line and third line because one's personal study teaches one to share with others.

It is the duty of a school to disseminate esoteric knowledge because there is no greater gift to bring to people than the knowledge of their selves. There are certain things that one can learn only through teaching, and second line of work is designed so that the students in the school have an opportunity to teach. Various cultures are taking root here, asserting themselves. It is our duty not only to remember ourselves but to transfer what we learn to the school. Self-remembering is first line; translating it is third line.

For new students, it is right to think mainly about first line. After one assimilates the system, one can share with other students. If one is working at one's highest level, the third line of work always encompasses the first line, for self-remembering must accompany one's actions.

One's evolution is directly related to one's ability to curb subjective thinking. Objective knowledge is not personal, although its verification is. Fragments of objective knowledge are not opinions, they are facts. Objective knowledge is mathematical, because if knowledge cannot be mathematical it can be only relatively true. Knowledge cannot be a substitute for self-remembering.

The longer one is in the school, the more is expected of one. The ability to contribute to third line of work increases. When one meets a school, third line is one's weakest line, which is right. One is intended to receive support from others much as an infant must be nourished when it comes into the world. Later, one can share information with one's fellow students, which is second line of work. Still later, third line of work begins as one starts contributing to the school. Steadily, the amount of third line work required of one increases.

Second and third lines of work must always include first line of work, that is, self-remembering. If one is working with another student, one must continue one's attempts to be present. Formatory mind assumes that one is to lay aside the first line of work when one proceeds with the second.

What did George Gurdjieff mean by sincerity?
To be truly sincere is to value self-remembering above all, and to be grateful to be assisted by outside forces. Mr. Ouspensky said the system is always in need of refinement. Our school has refined the system by focusing on the idea of self-remembering, and not becoming lost among the many ideas the system gives us. Less is more.

The growth of our school has always been slow, and that is healthy. I don't think the school could ever take in a large number of people at once because it would be too different from what we have experienced. We are turtles. Often, all one can do for the school is be present and patient. Although we live in an age of instant gratification, we do not live for quick results.

Vanity thinks that some people are not as worthy of respect as others. We are a large school and it is difficult to know everyone's name. One way to overcome this limitation is to respect whomever one meets. Although we are in different lifetimes, we all have the same gift and are part of Influence C's family. They love all of us; let us try to do the same.

We will grow old together, and you will understand the whole play of your life in the school only at the end of your life. Only the tragedy of this century could wring a school out of higher forces.

Schools are not for partial awakening. One must remember that the school exists to produce higher centers—try to wish for that more than anything else. Long ago I said that one has to give it everything and make consistent efforts throughout one's entire life.

Because the school has gone beyond the system to a certain extent, the great minds of antiquity are introduced to our meetings, as their teachings can now contribute to the emotionality of the work knowledge. William Shakespeare said, "And this above all, to thine own self be true." How can so vital a statement be absent from one's life?

We have accepted school in the form in which it has come. The system has shortcomings, but we cannot fault it, because it works. There will always be difficult years, some more so than others. I don't think about next year, or the last. Dwelling upon the past, or anticipating the future, one bypasses the present, and the present is where one's opportunities are.

My dear friends. You are in a critical situation. We live in a brutal universe where souls are endlessly driven from vessel to vessel. The gods have entered your life to enable you to escape this vicious cycle. Immortality is within your grasp. Firmly grip your aim to awaken and do not be distracted by anything. You are not alone; remember I love you, now and forever—*Robert.*

GLOSSARY

This Glossary provides brief descriptions of the special meanings that certain terms have acquired in the teaching of Robert Burton. More complete descriptions of most of them can be found in *In Search of the Miraculous*, *The Fourth Way* and *The Psychology of Man's Possible Evolution*, all by Peter Ouspensky. Special attention has been paid to those instances where Mr. Burton's emphasis differs slightly from that of Mr. Ouspensky. Readers who are familiar with the terminology of the Fourth Way are therefore advised to view the entries in this Glossary more as addenda to Mr. Ouspensky's presentation than as complete descriptions in themselves. At the same time, it is hoped that enough information is presented here to enable those who are not familiar with the Fourth Way to understand the essence of Mr. Burton's ideas.

References to other terms in the Glossary are indicated by SMALL CAPITALS.

ABSOLUTE, THE. The totality of everything that exists or could exist on all levels, in all worlds, and at all times; more specifically, the consciousness and understanding which exist at that level and thus comprise the highest possible intelligence.

ACCIDENT. Events that happen to a person and are neither a result of their own previous actions nor the direct result of conscious intention.

ACCIDENT, LAW OF. The influence of ACCIDENT on a person, in contrast to such influences as cause and effect, fate, and conscious will.

ACCOUNTS, keeping. The practice, centered especially in the JACK and QUEEN OF HEARTS, of remembering real or imagined wrongs and allowing one's reactions to others to be affected by them.

ACCUMULATORS. Storage locations for energy within the human MACHINE. Each CENTER has two associated accumulators that supply energy alternately. They are all replenished from a single large, or main, accumulator.

ACTIVE FORCE. First force: that which initiates a change or action.

ALCHEMY. (1) The degree of refinement of an IMPRESSION; the quality of the energy associated with an impression. (2) A characteristic of ESSENCE referring to one's capacity to be sensitive to the refinement of impressions.

In general, more refined impressions reflect higher, more conscious energy; they possess greater harmony, beauty and order. The alchemical metals of lead, copper, silver and gold refer to four levels of alchemy. The process of changing lead into gold is the process of making coarser impressions into finer ones. This can be done externally in one's environment and actions, internally by developing sensitivity to impressions in one's essence, and psychologically by BEING PRESENT to impressions and so experiencing them more fully.

ASCENDING OCTAVE. An octave in which there is growth from the more mechanical to the more intentional or conscious, for example, pieces of wood being given form and purpose by being made into a table. Ascending octaves are characterized by the need for effort, especially at the two INTERVALS.

ASTRAL BODY. The first metaphysical body that a person can create. It is capable of existing independently of the physical body.

BEING. The accumulated mass or effect of direct experience; more specifically, in relation to awakening, one's ability to experience, and participate consciously in, one's own life. In Robert Burton's teaching this is equivalent to one's ability to remember oneself.

A person who has accumulated experience in a particular area, as opposed to merely acquiring knowledge about it, is said to have being in that area. People who have being in cooking, for example, are able to do more than follow a recipe; they can engage many sides of themselves in the preparation of food, and so do it more creatively.

BEING PRESENT. The practice of paying attention to one's immediate environment, both externally and internally, without IMAGINATION or IDENTIFICATION.

BODY TYPE. A system, described by Rodney Collin and elaborated by Robert Burton, which classifies all human machines according to seven basic types. It links the cosmos of an individual to the cosmos of the solar system by establishing a link between the endocrine glands of the human body and the visible celestial bodies of the solar system, after which the types are named. Typically, an individual's physical and psychological characteristics can be described as a combination of two types, according to a definite progression. This progression, also referred to as the circulation of types, begins with the lunar type, then proceeds to the venusian, the mercurial, the saturnine, the martial and the jovial before returning to the lunar. The seventh type, the solar, exists separately from this progression and can be found in combination with any of the other types. The progression of types is also seen in the way in which a person may develop characteristics of the type ahead to balance or minimize weaknesses of the type behind. See *The Theory of Celestial Influence* by Rodney Collin for more complete descriptions.

BUFFER. (1) A psychological mechanism that prevents one from experiencing the reality of the present moment and seeing one's true mechanical condition; in particular, a mechanism by which FALSE PERSONALITY protects one's imaginary picture of oneself. (2) To use a buffer, as in "buffering an unpleasant situation."

CENTERS. The different independent intelligences or brains that exist for a human being. Four of these are present in all people: the instinctive center, the moving center, the emotional center and the intellectual center. Each of these centers is further divided into an instinctive, a moving, an emotional and an intellectual part. The parts are distinguished by the kind of attention that manifests in them. The intellectual parts are characterized by intentional effort to hold and direct attention. The emotional parts function when attention is drawn to and held by something. The moving and instinctive parts function automatically and without awareness, and are sometimes referred to together as the mechanical part of a center. This division can be carried one level further, to the instinctive, moving, emotional and intellectual parts of each part.

Centers, and their parts, are also divided into positive and negative halves. The positive half affirms and leads one toward things that seem beneficial to that part of that center. The negative half denies and leads one away from things that seem harmful or dangerous to that part of that center.

All of this is represented in the deck of playing cards. Each suit represents a center: clubs, the instinctive center; spades, the moving center; hearts, the emotional center; and diamonds, the intellectual center. The face cards represent the parts: the jacks, the mechanical parts; the queens, the emotional parts; and the kings, the intellectual parts. The numbered cards represent the parts of the parts: the eight, nine and ten being the mechanical, emotional and intellectual parts of the king; the five, six and seven the corresponding parts of the queen; and the two, three and four the parts of the jack. The ace represents the center as a whole.

In addition to these four lower centers, there is also the sex center, which is a source of higher energy that can be used for such things as procreation, artistic expression and awakening, and two HIGHER CENTERS: the higher emotional and higher intellectual centers. The two higher centers exist separately from the machine and manifest in higher states of consciousness. They can be considered to be the functions of the soul.

CENTER OF GRAVITY. The tendency in ESSENCE to relate to the world predominantly on the basis of attitudes that characterize a particular CENTER, and more specifically a part, and a part of a part, of a center. People usually favor their center of gravity over other parts of their MACHINE; its needs are unconsciously given a higher priority, and they tend to react from its point of view whether or not that is appropriate to the circumstances.

CHIEF FEATURE. A person's most strongly expressed FEATURE. As the core of FALSE PERSONALITY, it determines the fundamental way in which people view themselves and the world, and affects virtually all of their actions. Other features in a person's personality serve to support the chief feature and provide BUFFERS for it.

COLLIN, RODNEY. A student of Peter Ouspensky. He founded a school in Mexico following Ouspensky's death and taught throughout Latin America until his own death in 1956. His books, especially *The Theory of Celestial Influence,* have had a significant influence on Robert Burton's teaching.

CONSCIOUS BEING. A person who has achieved at least the level of MAN NUMBER FIVE and so has created higher bodies and developed a state of uninterrupted consciousness independent of the physical body. The term is used to refer to such beings both before and after the death of the physical body.

CONSCIOUS SHOCK, FIRST. Self-remembering, particularly as it applies to BEING PRESENT to and transforming IMPRESSIONS. The term is taken from the "Food Diagrams" in *In Search of the Miraculous* and *The Fourth Way,* where this effort is described as the SHOCK needed to initiate the digestion of impressions.

CONSCIOUS SHOCK, SECOND. The effort by which NEGATIVE EMOTIONS are transformed into positive emotions; the TRANSFORMATION OF SUFFERING. The term is taken from the "Food Diagrams" in *In Search of the Miraculous* and *The Fourth Way,* where this effort is described as the SHOCK that bridges the MI-FA INTERVAL in the octave of digestion of impressions and the SI-DO INTERVAL in the octave of the digestion of food.

CONSCIOUS TEACHING. A teaching directed by a CONSCIOUS BEING.

CONSCIOUSNESS. The ability to use attention to be aware. Consciousness can be measured in terms of what one is aware of, how long that awareness can be sustained, and how deep or profound the awareness is.

CRYSTALLIZATION. The process of psychological characteristics becoming fixed and permanent. More specifically, wrong crystallization refers to someone who has become set in mechanical patterns that are incompatible with awakening, while right or correct crystallization refers to someone who has made HIGHER CENTERS permanent within themselves.

DENYING FORCE. SECOND FORCE, seen more from the point of view of that which opposes or provides resistance to the FIRST FORCE.

DEPUTY STEWARD. A group of 'I's, larger than OBSERVING 'I' and smaller than a STEWARD, that observes the MACHINE and attempts to direct it in accordance with the aim to awaken.

DESCENDING OCTAVE. An octave in which manifestations proceed from the more conscious and flexible to the more rigid and mechanical, with a resulting loss of possibilities. Descending octaves have a momentum of their own and normally require little external effort. INTERVALS manifest more as places where there is an opportunity to interrupt or deviate the octave with an external SHOCK than as places where additional energy is required to keep the octave going.

DIVIDED ATTENTION. An intentional effort to be aware of two or more things simultaneously, in contrast with IDENTIFICATION, in which attention is focussed on only one thing. More specifically, divided attention often refers to self-remembering as an effort to be simultaneously aware of one's environment and of oneself within that environment.

DOMINANCE. A FEATURE to which order and control are major concerns. Externally, it may manifest as an ability to organize and direct others; directed internally, it causes a person to appear reserved, self-controlled and slow to act.

EMOTIONAL CENTER. The intelligence in a human MACHINE that is expressed as feelings and emotions.

EMOTIONAL PART. The PART OF A CENTER in which attention is held by a stimulus. In the positive half, this is experienced as pleasure, enjoyment and attraction; in the negative half, as discomfort, dislike and repulsion.

ESSENCE. The qualities of a human MACHINE that are inherent at birth, such as physical characteristics, BODY TYPE, CENTER OF GRAVITY and ALCHEMY. In most people, essence develops only during the first six or seven years of their lives, after which it is largely covered by FALSE PERSONALITY. Consequently, an experience of essence is often accompanied by a sense of childlike freedom and lightheartedness. However, in the path of awakening taught by Robert Burton, essence must be educated and developed beyond this childlike state.

EXERCISE, LISTENING. The practice of bringing attention to the sounds in one's environment as a means of BEING PRESENT and DIVIDING ATTENTION.

EXERCISE, LOOKING. The practice of shifting attention from one IMPRESSION to another approximately every three seconds, allowing enough time to take in the impression but changing one's focus before IMAGINATION or IDENTIFICATION occur.

EXTERNAL CONSIDERATION. The practice of considering one's relation to others from a point of view that places equal importance on oneself and others, and is in that sense external to oneself. More specifically, it sometimes refers to the fact that when one is practicing external consideration one will usually be more considerate of others.

FALSE PERSONALITY. A person's imaginary picture of himself, together with all the psychological mechanisms that are necessary to protect that picture. It develops in childhood in response to the pressures to receive adult approval and to behave in a socially acceptable way, but soon grows beyond its original role of protecting ESSENCE and acquires a life of its own. In the end, it completely dominates the lives of most people with a network of attitudes and patterns of behavior that are contrary to their true nature in essence.

FEAR. A FEATURE that has at its roots feelings of insecurity and powerlessness. It usually manifests as timidity in action and exaggerated concern about possibly harmful or dangerous consequences.

FEATURE. Fundamental attitudes in personality about oneself and one's relation to the world, along with all the psychological mechanisms that are needed to support and express those attitudes. In Robert Burton's teaching the principal features are vanity, power, dominance, nonexistence, greed, tramp, fear, naïvete, willfulness and lunatic. In each person, one of these is the chief feature, one or two others are strongly expressed, and there are traces of the remaining features.

FEMININE DOMINANCE. The largely unseen attitudes, mostly about the way things should be, that cause people to feel compelled to act in socially acceptable ways. It is feminine in the sense that a child usually acquires it from its mother during the process of learning acceptable behavior. Examples of attitudes that make up feminine dominance would include feelings of obligation toward others, expectations of others' behavior in relation to oneself, and the conviction that the world is essentially just and that one should be treated justly.

FIRST FORCE. The force or element that initiates a change or action.

FIRST-LINE WORK. Efforts made to promote one's own awakening; work on oneself.

FIRST STATE. The state of consciousness ordinarily called sleep.

FORCES, THREE. The three elements or energies that must be present before any real change or action can occur. The first, or active, force initiates the action. The second force, also called passive or denying force, in some way provides resistance for the first force; for example, it may be what is acted upon. The presence of the third, or neutralizing, force allows the opposition between the first two forces to be resolved. It is sometimes seen as the medium in which the other two forces act, and sometimes as an additional factor or influence. Together the three forces are called a triad, and before it is possible to achieve a desired result, the right triad, or combination of forces, must be found.

FORMATORY MIND. In general, automatic, unthinking responses according to fixed patterns or forms; more specifically, the automatic activity of the MECHANICAL PART of the INTELLECTUAL CENTER.

FOUR LOWER CENTERS. The instinctive, moving, emotional and intellectual centers.

FOURTH WAY. The path of awakening practiced by George Gurdjieff, Peter Ouspensky and their followers, including Robert Burton.

FRICTION. In general, the internal struggle between the part of a person that wishes to awaken and the mechanical patterns of behavior that interfere with that aim. More specifically, friction refers to external events that precipitate that struggle, particularly when suffering is involved.

FUNCTIONS. CENTERS, with an emphasis more on their mechanical-ness than on their intelligence.

GESTATION. The period during which a person is working to awaken. The emphasis is on the idea that something is developing inter-nally that, when mature, will enable one to experience HIGHER CENTERS.

GOOD HOUSEHOLDER. A person who values things according to their true worth; also the values held by such people. In particular, good householders make efforts to care for themselves, their belongings, their environment and their relations to others.

GREED. A FEATURE characterized by an exaggerated valuation for external things. It causes people to wish particularly to accumu-late and possess things that others consider to be valuable as a means of asserting their own worth.

GURDJIEFF, GEORGE. An Armenian Greek born in the late nineteenth century who traveled extensively throughout the Near East and Central Asia to collect the esoteric knowledge that forms the basis of the FOURTH WAY. He escaped from Russia in the confusion following the Revolution and eventually settled in Paris, where he continued to teach until his death in 1949.

HIGHER CENTERS. The higher emotional and higher intellectual centers. The higher emotional center is capable of perceiving the connectedness of all things and is the seat of conscious love and compassion. The higher intellectual center perceives the laws that govern all things and is the seat of conscious wisdom.

HIGHER SCHOOL. A reference to the idea that even after they no longer possess physical bodies, conscious beings continue to evolve under the guidance of yet higher beings.

HYDROGEN. In general, the smallest unit of anything that still retains all of its physical, metaphysical, psychological and cosmic properties; more specifically, the energy associated with an IMPRESSION as it affects a human MACHINE. Higher hydrogens are quick, light energies that are associated with perception and consciousness; lower hydrogens are heavy, coarse, dense energies that evoke dullness and negativity.

'I's. The short-lived thoughts, emotions and sensations that one takes to be the expression of oneself in the moment they occur, with emphasis on their expression in words in the INTELLECTUAL CENTER. People have a tremendous number of 'I's, many of which are contradictory, but ordinarily they fail to notice this.

IDENTIFICATION. (1) The state in which all of a person's attention is focused on a single thing to the exclusion of anything else; the opposite of SEPARATION. (2) The tendency, especially of FALSE PERSONALITY, to place one's sense of identity in things that are external to one's true self.

IMAGINATION. (1) The state in which a person's attention is devoted to things that are not actually present, often to the complete exclusion of awareness of the immediate environment; the opposite of BEING PRESENT. (2) The condition of believing something to be true that is not true, often used in the phrase, "to be in imagination about."

IMPRESSION. In general, any thought, feeling or sensation; more specifically, perceptions that are received through the senses.

INFLUENCE A. Influences on a person that arise as a consequence of life on earth. In general, these influences include such things as the desires for food, shelter, rest and sex; relations between parents, children, spouses and friends; and the influence of society and culture. More specifically, in the modern world the emphasis is on the desire for material possessions and social position.

INFLUENCE B. Influences on a person, such as religion and esotericism, that are not directly connected with life on earth and that point toward other forms of existence. Such influences originate with CONSCIOUS BEINGS but cease to qualify as INFLUENCE C as soon as they lose their direct connection to a conscious source.

INFLUENCE C. (1) The direct influence of CONSCIOUS BEINGS. (2) Conscious beings without physical bodies who are working directly to assist people who are trying to awaken.

INFRA-SEX. The use of sex energy for purposes that are not connected with procreation or regeneration; for example, its use for personal gratification or to influence others.

INNER CIRCLE. People in a school of awakening who share a higher LEVEL OF BEING and understanding, and so are working toward a common aim.

INNER CONSIDERING. Considering one's relation to others from a point of view that places oneself at the center and considers others only in relation to that center. Inner considering leads to excessive concern over the way one appears to others and the way they react to one, at times to the point of producing an incapacitating state of fear and confusion.

INSTINCTIVE CENTER. The intelligence in a human MACHINE that controls, or manifests as, instinctive functions, such as the activity of the senses, intuition, the growth of the body, the distribution of energy within the body, and so on.

INSTINCTIVE PART. The part of a CENTER that functions most automatically and satisfies the most basic needs of the center.

INTELLECTUAL CENTER. The intelligence in a human MACHINE that manifests as thought and reason.

INTELLECTUAL PART. The part of a CENTER that functions when an effort is made to control and direct attention. It is the highest intelligence in that center.

INTENTIONAL INSINCERITY. The practice, in order to further one's aim, of saying something that is not strictly true in circumstances where it will not cause real harm to anyone.

INTERVAL. In general, the points in an OCTAVE where the movement between events slows and the octave may deviate. The word is most frequently used to refer to the times when extra effort is needed to advance a project, and to the times of confusion and doubt that characterize a loss of direction in a person's efforts to awaken.

JACK. The MECHANICAL PART of a CENTER.

JOVIAL. The BODY TYPE that lies between the martial and the lunar in the circulation of types. Its MAXIMUM ATTRACTION is the mercurial.

KING. The INTELLECTUAL PART of a CENTER.

KING OF HEARTS. The INTELLECTUAL PART of the EMOTIONAL CENTER. It is called the gateway to higher centers because it can, if properly trained, experience life in a non-literal, symbolic way very close to the experience of the higher emotional center.

KING OF DIAMONDS. The INTELLECTUAL PART of the INTELLECTUAL CENTER. It is the seat of logical, intentional thought directed toward a specific goal.

LATERAL OCTAVE. A smaller octave begun within a larger octave to overcome an INTERVAL in the larger octave. For example, an interval in a construction project might manifest as running out of material, in which case a lateral octave would be needed to find a supplier, place an order, and have the material delivered. Especially with psychological octaves, such as those associated with self-remembering, there is a danger that one will lose sight of the main octave and, by following the lateral octave, deviate from the original aim.

LEVEL OF BEING. Degree of consciousness. People with higher levels of being are more conscious, more awake, than those with lower levels of being; consequently they are better able to remember themselves.

LIFE. Human activity not associated with a school of awakening. In particular, life people are those people who are not in a school, and life influences are those influences on a student that come from outside the school.

LINES OF WORK, THREE. Work for oneself (FIRST LINE), work for and with others (SECOND LINE), and work for one's teacher or school (THIRD LINE). Robert Burton's teaching emphasizes the need for balance among these lines.

LIVES, MANY. The various lifetimes through which a RECURRING soul may pass.

LIVES, NINE. The nine lifetimes through which an evolving soul may pass before escaping the physical plane of existence on the ninth.

LOWER CENTERS. The instinctive, moving, emotional and intellectual centers, sometimes together with the sex center.

LUNAR. The BODY TYPE that lies between the jovial and the venusian in the circulation of types. Its MAXIMUM ATTRACTION is the saturnine.

LUNATIC. A FEATURE that is based on an inability to recognize the relative value of things. It manifests as a tendency to attach too much importance to relatively trivial matters and too little importance to truly significant ones.

MACHINE, THE. The physical body, and the FOUR LOWER CENTERS that comprise it, from the point of view that all their activity occurs automatically and mechanically in response to stimuli.

MAGNETIC CENTER. That portion of a person's personality that is attracted to INFLUENCES B and may eventually lead him to seek a school of awakening and INFLUENCE C.

MAN NUMBER ONE. A person whose CENTER OF GRAVITY is in the MOVING or INSTINCTIVE CENTERS.

MAN NUMBER TWO. A person whose CENTER OF GRAVITY is in the EMOTIONAL CENTER. Men number two are dominated by likes and dislikes.

MAN NUMBER THREE. A person whose CENTER OF GRAVITY is in the intellectual center. Reason, logic and ideas are more important to men number three than they are to others.

MAN NUMBER FOUR. Specifically, a person in a school of awakening; more generally, a person who is working to awaken and who understands himself well enough to begin to separate from his mechanical CENTER OF GRAVITY and replace it with a "center of gravity" in the work. This means that men number four react to stimuli on the basis of their relation to their aim to awaken, rather than on the basis of one of the LOWER CENTERS.

MAN NUMBER FIVE. A person whose CENTER OF GRAVITY is in the HIGHER EMOTIONAL CENTER. Men number five are fully objective about themselves.

MAN NUMBER SIX. A person whose CENTER OF GRAVITY is in the HIGHER INTELLECTUAL CENTER. Men number six see both themselves and the world objectively.

MAN NUMBER SEVEN. A person who has achieved all that is possible for a human being. Men number seven have complete unity and possess will and consciousness that are independent of any of their FUNCTIONS.

MARTIAL. The BODY TYPE that lies between the saturnine and the jovial in the circulation of types. Its MAXIMUM ATTRACTION is the venusian.

MASTER. HIGHER CENTERS, especially from the point of view of their ability to observe and direct the LOWER CENTERS.

MAXIMUM ATTRACTION. The tendency for there to be a particularly strong attraction between BODY TYPES that are three types apart in the circulation of types. These types are opposites in some respects and the relationship between them is often stormy.

MECHANICAL PART. The moving and instinctive parts of a CENTER.

MEETINGS. The regular gatherings of members of the Fellowship of Friends to discuss the ideas of the SYSTEM and their application to members' efforts to awaken. Typically, a meeting is lead by a relatively senior member, who asks for questions to which all present share "angles of thought."

MERCURIAL. The BODY TYPE that lies between the venusian and the saturnine in the circulation of types. Its MAXIMUM ATTRACTION is the jovial.

MICROCOSMOS. A human being considered as a cosmos, that is, as an image of the fundamental pattern of the universe.

'MI-FA' INTERVAL. The first interval in an ascending OCTAVE, for example, the interval between preparing plans for a project and beginning the actual work. In general, the 'mi-fa' interval is easier to overcome than the 'SI-DO'.

MOVING CENTER. The intelligence in a human MACHINE that orients it in space and directs its external movements.

MOVING PART. The part of CENTER that functions automatically without attention but is more externally directed than the IN-STINCTIVE PART. It can often be seen as using or manipulating the material provided by the instinctive part.

NAÏVETE. A FEATURE characterized by a relative inability to see the unpleasant aspects of life and the potential harmful or negative consequences of one's actions.

NEGATIVE EMOTIONS. Any of the emotions, such as anger, jealousy, indignation, self-pity and boredom, that are negative in charac-ter. They are the principal BUFFERS used by FEATURES and FALSE PERSONALITY to prevent a person from seeing and accepting their situation objectively. Because negative emotions are always based on IMAGINATION and IDENTIFICATION, it is possible to eliminate them through long, hard work on oneself, and this is one of the major emphases of Robert Burton's teaching.

NEGATIVITY. Any negative expression in one of the FOUR LOWER CENTERS, especially when accompanied by a NEGATIVE EMOTION. Negative or threatening postures, complaining and gossiping are examples of negativity.

NEUTRALIZING FORCE. Third force, with an emphasis on its role as that which resolves the tension between the FIRST and SECOND FORCES.

NICOLL, MAURICE. A student of Peter Ouspensky who lead groups of his own in England during the 1940s. He wrote a number of books, among which Robert Burton has especially acknowledged the value of the *Psychological Commentaries on the Teaching of Gurdjieff and Ouspensky.*

NON-EXISTENCE. A FEATURE characterized by a lack of valuation for oneself and often by a relative lack of internal activity, resulting in a tendency to live through others.

OBSERVING 'I'. A small group of 'I's that observes the machine from the point of view of the SYSTEM; the beginning of SELF-OBSERVATION and the first stage in awakening.

OCTAVE. Often used to refer to an activity or project as a reminder of its connection to the Law of OCTAVES.

OCTAVES, LAW OF. A description of the way in which any sequence of events eventually loses its force or direction. Also known as the Law of Seven, this law is embodied in both Gurdjieff's Enneagram and in the major musical scale. In the latter, each note corresponds to an event in the sequence, with the half-steps between mi and fa, and between si and do representing intervals where the progress from one event to the next slows and a deviation or interruption will occur unless a shock is received from outside the octave itself. Octaves may be ascending, that is, proceeding from more mechanical and limited manifestations to more intentional, conscious and flexible manifestations, or descending, in which case the manifestations proceed from those that are more conscious and have more potential to those that are more mechanical and fixed.

OUSPENSKY, PETER. A Russian student of George Gurdjieff. He escaped to the West with Gurdjieff during the Russian Revolution, but later parted with him to establish a school of his own in London, where he taught until his death in 1947. His books, *In Search of the Miraculous, The Fourth Way* and *The Psychology of Man's Possible Evolution,* are the basis of Robert Burton's teaching.

PARTS OF CENTERS. The subdivisions of the FOUR LOWER CENTERS.

PASSIVE FORCE. SECOND FORCE, seen more from the point of view of that which is acted upon by the FIRST FORCE.

PHOTOGRAPH. An observation of the state or behavior of oneself or another person; also, to direct the attention of another person to his state or behavior.

PLAY, THE. A sequence of events seen from the point of view that all events occur under the guidance and control of higher forces, or INFLUENCE C, who in this sense are the authors of "the play."

POWER. A FEATURE characterized by concern over the ability to direct, control or influence the activities of others. People with this feature are usually extroverted, and tend to be somewhat manipulative and political in outlook.

QUEEN. The emotional part of a CENTER.

QUEEN OF HEARTS. The emotional part of the EMOTIONAL CENTER. It is characterized by extreme and frequently uncontrolled emotions.

RAY OF CREATION. A representation of the universe as consisting of worlds of lower levels contained within worlds of higher levels. The Ray begins with the Absolute and ends with the earth and the moon. The worlds below (or within) the Absolute are referred to by the numbers 3, 6, 12, 24, 48 and 96, reflecting the increasing complexity and mechanicality of existence in each world.

RECURRENCE. The theory that souls which do not evolve during one lifetime will be reborn into essentially the same life. This theory differs from the theory of reincarnation in that it does not suppose a migration of souls from one form of existence to another.

RELATIVITY. The practice of considering something, such as an event or another person, from different points of view. It is an opposite to IDENTIFICATION, in which all awareness is trapped in a single point of view.

RIGHT WORK OF CENTERS. The condition in which each center and each part of each center responds only to the stimuli that are appropriate to it; contrasted with WRONG WORK OF CENTERS.

RULING FACULTY. In general, a man's highest understanding about his actions and their consequences; more specifically, HIGHER CENTERS from the point of view of their ability to guide the manifestations of the MACHINE.

SATURNINE. The BODY TYPE that lies between the mercurial and the martial in the circulation of types. Its MAXIMUM ATTRACTION is the lunar.

SCALE. The ability to view an event or experience from larger and smaller perspectives. It is especially useful to combat IDENTIFICATION. For example, faced with the prospect of a difficult encounter, a person might focus on the immediate environment (in which the encounter is not yet occurring) or attempt to view the situation in terms of a full year, thus rendering it insignificant. HIGHER CENTERS enable a person to apply scale by experiencing life from the perspective of higher worlds, in comparison with which one's ordinary existence may be seen as an illusion.

SECOND FORCE. The force or element that balances the FIRST FORCE in the sense that it opposes it or is acted upon by it.

SECOND-LINE WORK. Efforts made to help other members of one's school; work with other students.

SECOND STATE. The ordinary state of consciousness of most people, in which they act and react with little or no awareness of themselves, that is, without self-remembering. For this reason it is called "sleep."

SELF, THE. HIGHER CENTERS, particularly as seen from the point of view of their independence of anything external to them.

SELF-OBSERVATION. The practice of being aware of one's internal functions at the same time as one is aware of one's actions and environment; the aspect of self-remembering that involves being aware of the manifestations of one's MACHINE.

SEPARATION. The practice of maintaining a sense of self separate from one's actions, environment or experience; the aspect of self-remembering that involves a withdrawal of a part of one's attention from one's experiences and using it to be aware of that within one which registers, or is aware of, those experiences. The emphasis is on the fact that the part which registers the experience is not directly involved in or affected by the experience.

SEX CENTER. A source of higher energy (hydrogen 12) in the human MACHINE. Because the energy of the sex center manifests through the other centers, the sex center can only be directly observed in higher states of consciousness.

SHOCKS. In general, anything that occurs at an interval in an OCTAVE to cause the octave to continue, with or without deviation; in particular, events that interrupt a person's usual state.

'SI-DO' INTERVAL. The interval at the end of an ascending OCTAVE, for example, the struggle to bring a project to a final state of completion and clear up all the loose ends.

SOLAR. A BODY TYPE that does not belong to the circulation of types and so can be found in combination with any of the other types. It has no MAXIMUM ATTRACTION.

STEWARD. A group of 'I's that grows out of DEPUTY STEWARD and is usually able to observe the MACHINE and control it in accordance with the aim to awaken.

SYSTEM, THE. The ideas of George Gurdjieff, particularly as expounded by Peter Ouspensky and his principal followers.

TABLE OF HYDROGENS. A table, described in detail in *In Search of the Miraculous* and *The Fourth Way*, which relates energies, materials, objects and all other manifestations to the cosmic level from which they come, according to their HYDROGENS.

TAPES. Pre-existing, automatic responses to a stimulus, especially those which manifest as 'I's in the INTELLECTUAL CENTER.

THIRD FORCE. The force or element whose presence allows the tension between the FIRST and SECOND FORCES to be resolved.

THIRD-LINE WORK. Efforts to serve one's teacher, one's school, conscious beings, or the work of awakening in general.

THIRD STATE. A state of consciousness, induced by efforts of self-remembering, in which a man SEPARATES from his personality and observes himself objectively. It is characterized by self-awareness and an absence of IDENTIFICATION and IMAGINATION, but lacks the ability to be fully objective about the external world.

TRAMP. A FEATURE characterized by an inability to value things, both physical and psychological. To a tramp feature, nothing matters much; there is no need to get excited; and it is fine to "go with the flow" of things.

TRANSFORMATION OF IMPRESSIONS. The practice of using self-remembering to bring attention to the impressions one receives and so make them more emotional and raise them to a higher level.

TRANSFORMATION OF SUFFERING. The practice of SEPARATING from suffering and experiencing it in such a way that it can be accepted freely and without NEGATIVITY. In its highest expression, transformation involves the activity of HIGHER CENTERS and leads to powerful experiences of increased consciousness.

TRUE PERSONALITY. Personality based on an understanding of one's ESSENCE and the needs of one's work, and which therefore serves and promotes both essence and the work; opposed to FALSE PERSONALITY, which is contrary to the true needs of essence and the work.

UNNECESSARY SUFFERING. Suffering that could be avoided by more intelligent behavior; in particular, suffering that is a result of IMAGINATION or IDENTIFICATION and so would not occur in higher states of consciousness.

VANITY. A FEATURE characterized by concern about oneself, and particularly about how one appears to others. It may manifest internally as self-pity or self-deprecation and externally in attempts to attract the attention of others.

VENUSIAN. The BODY TYPE that lies between the lunar and the mercurial in the circulation of types. Its MAXIMUM ATTRACTION is the martial.

VERIFY. To convince oneself of the truth of the ideas of the SYSTEM through direct personal experience. The emphasis is on the idea that more is required than intellectual activity.

VOLUNTARY SUFFERING. The practice of creating relatively minor discomfort or inconvenience for oneself in order to interrupt one's usual state and remind one to remember oneself.

WAY, THE. The particular path of awakening that is embodied in a school. To be "on the way" implies that a person has made a commitment to awakening above other concerns of life and has a grasp of the main ideas of the SYSTEM.

WAY OF LOVE. A teaching in which the teacher uses relatively gentle methods to encourage and support his students' efforts. The emphasis is more on developing new capacities to eventually supplant old patterns of behavior than on destroying those patterns directly.

WAY OF DENIAL. A teaching in which students must begin by giving up IDENTIFICATIONS in order to leave space for higher states. The teacher frequently administers relatively harsh SHOCKS to attack the student's FALSE PERSONALITY.

WILLFULNESS. A FEATURE based on feelings of helplessness, which are expressed as a desire to hold on to what one has and to resist change as the only means of avoiding being swept away by the flow of events.

WORK 'I's. 'I's that remind a person to make efforts to further his work to awaken.

WORLD 96, 48, 24, 12 and 6. The different levels in the RAY OF CREATION. In psychological terms, World 96 is the level of FALSE PERSONALITY; World 48, the level of TRUE PERSONALITY; World 24, the level of ESSENCE; World 12, the level of the HIGHER EMOTIONAL CENTER; and World 6, the level of the HIGHER INTELLECTUAL CENTER.

WRONG WORK OF CENTERS. The condition in which the FOUR LOWER CENTERS and their various parts routinely react to stimuli that are not appropriate to them. Examples include becoming emotional about balancing a check book, responding logically to another person's emotional distress, and fidgeting or feeling ill when experiencing unpleasant emotions. Such wrong work is the usual state of humanity.

THE FELLOWSHIP
OF FRIENDS

The Fellowship of Friends, a Fourth Way School in the tradition of Gurdjieff and Ouspensky, was founded by Robert Earl Burton. The Fellowship's main location is at Apollo, a community in the foothills of California's Sierra Nevada mountains. Teaching centers are maintained in major cities throughout the world, some of which are listed below:

Ahmedabad	Milan
Amsterdam	Moscow
Athens	New York
Berlin	Palo Alto
Brussels	Paris
Buenos Aires	Rome
Copenhagen	Sacramento
Dublin	San Francisco
Edinburgh	Saõ Paulo
Florence	St. Petersburg
Frankfurt	Sydney
London	Taipei
Los Angeles	Tel Aviv
Madrid	Tokyo
Mexico City	Toronto

For more information on the Fellowship, or details of membership, please call or write for the Fellowship center nearest you:

The Fellowship of Friends
Post Office Box 100
Oregon House, California 95962
(916) 692-2244

Aerial view in winter of Apollo, California. *Photography / James Klin*

Frederic Choisel

Robert Burton is the founder and spiritual leader of the Fellowship of Friends, a Fourth Way school in the Gurdjieff-Ouspensky tradition. He has practiced and taught his system for self-development to thousands of students around the world.

Printed in the United States
150623LV00001B/13/P